CHIHUAHUA

SMART OWNER'S GUIDE™

FROM THE EDITORS OF DOGFANCY MAGAZINE

CONTENTS

Chihuahua, a Smart Owner's Guide™
part of the Kennel Club Books® Interactive Series™
ISBN: 978-1-593787-64-6. ©2009

Kennel Club Books Inc., 40 Broad St., Freehold, NJ 07728. Printed in China.

*photographers include Isabelle Francias/BowTie Inc.; Tara Darling/BowTie Inc.;
Gina Cioli and Pamela Hunnicutt/BowTie Inc. Contributing writer: Barbara J. Andrews*

For CIP information, see page 176.

K9 EXPERT

So, you think you want the tiniest of dogs? Don't be fooled by the short legs and diminutive body of the Chihuahua. This breed is as much of a responsibility as any other dog.

Despite their cute size — weighing less than 6 pounds and standing 6 to 9 inches tall — and cute, cute faces, Chihuahuas need firm house rules and consistent training from the first day they go home with you. If you treat your Chi like a doll or toy, he's likely to turn into a dog who nips at strangers and a manipulator who runs your household.

It can be tough to tell your darling little dog "no" and mean it. But you have to. He needs to know that you're the boss and you're going to make him follow the rules. Stick with it, and he'll turn into a companion whose years with you will slip by so fast you won't believe it.

Once you've had a Chihuahua in your home, though, you'll likely always have one; or, you'll want to bring home a few more! Chis are full of energy and fun, and are extremely portable. You can take your Chi just about anywhere, tucked in a bag or even in a pocket. Then, when he's back at home with you, he'll revert to his watchdog mode by letting you know whenever someone approaches your house or apartment.

EDUCATION

If you're looking for an easygoing lap dog, this isn't the breed for you. Smart and tenacious, your Chihuahua will keep you on your toes. You'll need to redirect that intelligence and energy with regular walks, obedience training and perhaps a canine sport, such as agility or flyball. This isn't a sit-on-the-couch-all-day kind of dog.

But like a lap dog, your Chi will want lots of attention from you and plenty of contact. He won't happily stay in a crate all day, and of course, you can't leave him in the backyard unsupervised. A midday walk, doggie day care or another outlet will help keep him happy and healthy.

When you get home from work or an outing, be ready to take him outside for a pleasant stroll. Later, if you need to run errands, he'll want to be right there by your side. Need to take a break, sit outside a coffee shop and relax? Your Chihuahua will gladly keep you company. If you've socialized and trained him well, he will entertain everyone he meets — the barista, other coffee *afficionados* and anyone else you greet.

A few words of caution before you go to pick out your new Chi: Chihuahuas don't often mesh well with young children. But, if your children are older and know how to be careful around a tiny dog, things should be just fine. Your Chihuahua also needs a patient and consistent partner when it comes to housetraining. Be prepared to take some time to housetrain your Chi, and acknowledge and accept there will be accidents. Eventually, your tiny companion will learn where, when and how to take care of his potty business.

Remember: Just as your Chihuahua is willing to cooperate with you, you also have to

JOIN OUR ONLINE Club Chi™

With this Smart Owner's Guide™, you are well on your way to getting your Chihuahua diploma. But your Chi education doesn't end here. You're invited to join **Club Chi™ (DogChannel.com/Club-Chi)**, a FREE online site with lots of fun and instructive online features like:

◆ **forums, blogs** and **profiles** where you can connect with other Chi owners
◆ **downloadable charts** and **checklists** to help you be a smart and loving Chihuahua owner
◆ access to Chihuahua **e-cards** and **wallpapers**
◆ interactive **games**
◆ **quizzes** about dogs

The **Smart Owner's Guide** series and **Club Chi** are backed by the experts at DOG FANCY® magazine and DogChannel.com — who have been providing trusted and up-to-date information about dogs and dog lovers for more than 40 years. Log on and join the club today!

keep up your end of the deal. That means teaching your new canine pal you're in charge while giving him all the love, attention and care that he deserves, craves and needs. Together, you will make a mighty great team for many years to come.

Susan Chaney
Editor, DOG FANCY

CHAPTER 1

THE SECRET

You think they're cute, you're dying to cuddle one and you just love their darling, batlike ears. But, those nagging questions continue to haunt you: Do you have what it takes to take on the formidable challenge of owning the diminutive Chihuahua? Are you worthy of this tiny dog's extreme devotion and unyielding affection?

THE CHI CAN'T HELP IT

Chihuahua owner Roger Balettie from Austin, Texas, never saw himself as the typical Chihuahua companion. "I'll be honest: I originally wasn't that interested in getting a Chihuahua as a pet," Balettie says. "I had always grown up with big dogs and was leaning more toward getting one of those. However, once I got Bambi, I was hooked. I bought Nina one year later to keep Bambi company, and two Chis are certainly more fun than one!"

Anyone considering a Chihuahua must be prepared for both the wonderful and challenging aspects of Chi ownership. "Chihuahua owners must be ready to give a whole lot of attention to their dog," says Sharon Hermosillo, a breeder and former rescue

it's a Fact
You can expect your Chihuahua puppy to reach emotional maturity by 3 years old. Although socialization is most important in the weeks prior to 4 months, social exposure should continue throughout the dog's first year and into adulthood.

chairperson of the Chihuahua Club of America from San Jose, Calif.

Balettie agrees. "My Chis, at least, require a great deal of attention and affection," he says. "They are the perfect definition of a lap dog, wanting to be near me at all times, whether I'm watching television, working on the computer or fixing dinner." Balettie insists that such constant companionship is far from a negative aspect of owning a Chihuahua.

"Chis are so small that they don't overwhelm when they pounce into their favorite seating position," he says. "The affection they give in return for the attention they demand makes it all worth it." A Chihuahua certainly needs plenty of petting and affection daily!

JOIN OUR ONLINE Club Chi™

Meet other Chihuahua owners just like you. On our toy dog-forums, you can chat about your Chihuahua and ask other owners for advice on training, health issues and anything else about your favorite dog breed. Log onto **DogChannel.com/Club-Chi** for details!

Chihuahuas have a reputation for being clannish, unfriendly toward other dogs and suspicious of strangers. However, thanks to proper breeding, many of the more undesirable Chihuahua characteristics are a thing of the past. "The love and devotion that Chihuahuas express is so contrary to the stereotype that has been propagated over the years of Chihuahuas as 'yappy, little-old-lady dogs,'" Balettie says. "Fortunately, most of the more respectable Chihuahua breeders have bred out the obnoxious traits, leaving the sweet-tempered, affectionate dog as the standard for the Chihuahua today."

Whether or not a Chi is friendly and tolerant of strangers largely depends on how well he's been socialized. "People get a Chi and never take him anywhere, then wonder why he doesn't like anyone," Hermosillo says. "Chis are very sociable if you work with them." Hermosillo suggests taking a Chihuahua puppy with you everywhere and letting him meet a wide variety of people so he will become accustomed to people outside of his family.

What about other breeds? "Chis normally prefer their own kind — they really do love other Chihuahuas — but my daughter had a Chi and a German Shepherd Dog for four years and they were best friends," Hermosillo says. Surprisingly, most Chis enjoy cats. "Our Chis just love our cats," she says. "Of course, when my Chis all get together, they suddenly get very brave and gang up on the cats; but if they're playing one-on-one, Chis and cats generally do very well together."

With other pets, as well as people, socialization prevents poor social skills and some behavioral problems. The more a Chihuahua is exposed to people and animals alike, the more comfortable and agreeable he will

Chis make excellent watchdogs, but if you don't want them to bark at every stranger, you must socialize them, pronto!

become. While it may take more time for your Chihuahua to warm up to other members of the family, their love and affection is well worth the wait.

Chihuahuas certainly are not outdoor dogs. Some Chihuahuas enjoy a romp in the yard or the park, but they will be more than happy to come back inside and return to the comfort of a cozy couch cushion or, better yet, to snuggle beneath the quilts and pillows on your bed. If you're in bed too, that's even better. "They absolutely must live inside, and they prefer to be bed dogs," Hermosillo says.

Chihuahuas like nothing better than to be with you, by you or on you at all times. Nancy Robbins' Chihuahuas, Ishi-Boo and Pooh, are rarely far from her side. "They are usually both right there next to me or on me," says Robbins, from Suwanee, Ga. "Ninety-nine percent of the time I have one curled up under my shirt and the other at my side."

Furthermore, Chihuahuas require what some might call "excessive indulgence;" others might call it "spoiled rotten." That's one way of putting it. But who can resist those perky ears and glittering eyes? After Robbins moved into a new house, her 2-year-old male Chihuahua, Ishi-Boo, lined up a few new chores for his obliging human.

"Since we have lived here, you'll find Ishi-Boo insisting on being lifted into the bed at night or being lifted into the tub to lick up any water droplets I leave behind every morning," says Robbins, who admits she readily complies. Now that's service!

Balettie's Chis demand treats from a gourmet dog bakery and use their human as a comfy perch for watching television. In fact, Balettie's 2-year-old Chi, Nina, has a favorite place to spend her time: on her owner's shoulder!

"Whenever I sit down to watch television, Nina will race from where she happens to be at the time, fly from the ground onto my lap, and in one leap, land on my shoulder," he says. "If I were a pirate, she'd be my parrot."

An interest in catering to the often eccentric whims of a little dog is a must for a smart Chi owner.

The perfect owner for a Chi is someone who will shower his or her Chi with lots of love and attention.

Perhaps the most important characteristic of a smart Chihuahua owner — after a huge capacity for love — is a good sense of humor. Chihuahuas can be downright hilarious, and a good Chi owner appreciates, and even cherishes, their antics. Robbins' Chi, Ishi-Boo, quickly mastered the art of humor as a great way to get what he wants. "Ishi-Boo is a dancer," Robbins says. "He can walk the whole house on his hind legs with his front paws just swinging away, up and down as fast as he can paddle them. It gets him almost anything he wants from just about anybody."

Sometimes Chis are funny without intending to be. Balettie's Chi, Bambi, has taken her role as watchdog to an extreme. "In January, my father and I were watching one of the football playoff games when Bambi, who had been sitting next to me in a chair in the den, started staring at my father and growling," Balettie explains. "Now, you must understand, Bambi does not growl at anyone; she has a very calm disposition. Her growls, though, became louder and more insistent. Finally, my father and I both realized the object of her ire was not my father, but the timber wolf printed on his sweatshirt. From across the room, Bambi had seen this other 'dog' and wasn't happy about its presence. My father covered the wolf on the shirt and Bambi seemed satisfied. If he uncovered the wolf, Bambi would start growling again."

Get ready for a life filled with humor with your new Chihuahua.

A MATCH MADE IN HEAVEN?

Is a Chihuahua for you? Only you can decide. These guidelines will help you make that decision before you bring a new, little puppy into your home. Don't expect the road to be easy or emotion free. "An ideal Chihuahua owner needs to have patience with these little dogs because their need to love and be loved is an all-consuming crusade," Balettie says. "The return on the investment, though, is much greater than the demand on your time."

Are you ready to fall in love? "Anyone wanting something to love or wanting to be loved could own a Chihuahua," Robbins states. "I can't imagine any true animal person, given the opportunity to be around one long enough, not getting hooked on Chihuahuas. It doesn't take much for them to grab hold of your heartstrings, and they never let go."

Still thinking about a big dog? Or is the idea of a Chihuahua starting to grow on you? Be careful, you may just become the perfect Chihuahua owner.

LOOK BEFORE YOU SIT!

Chihuahuas have tons of self-esteem for their petite bodies, but they are tiny and can easily be injured if stepped on, closed into a door or fallen on by a wobbling toddler. Chi puppies are particularly delicate and have been known to break their legs if allowed to jump from high places, such as couches or tables. Just because your Chi

NOTABLE & QUOTABLE

It takes a special person to care for any animal, but it takes a very special person to take care of a Chihuahua. Anyone who is considering having a Chihuahua as a pet needs to know that having a Chihuahua is very much like taking care of a child.
— *John Re, Chi owner from Tampa, Fla.*

can get up on a couch doesn't mean he can get down safely. Chihuahuas also love to snuggle under blankets, pillows and cushions where they can't be seen. Loving family members can easily — and unintentionally — injure their beloved pets by walking, sitting or lying down on their Chi.

If you are considering bringing home a Chihuahua, you must be vigilant about his whereabouts at all times. "A new Chi owner needs to realize that these are tiny dogs, so being a little more careful about where they sit or step becomes a natural habit after a while," Balettie says. "Before sitting on a blanket or pillow, I always make sure one of my Chis isn't hiding." If you are thinking of bringing home a Chihuahua, you might as well start practicing: Look before you sit!

AMIGOS FOR SENIORS

Of all the potentially perfect, smart Chihuahua owners out there, seniors are among the best. Chis are ideal for older people who stay home a lot and who may not be particularly active. Unlike many other breeds, Chihuahuas can get plenty of exercise romping around a small space. As long as they are trained to eliminate in a convenient spot, Chis will be perfectly happy to stay inside all day snuggling beside their favorite person.

Chihuahuas are also low-maintenance in terms of care. They require minimal grooming and only a small supply of good food and water. As far as their high-maintenance reputation goes, that's the fun part; the Chihuahua's desire for constant attention and affection is a great remedy for loneliness or boredom, and a well-loved Chi will repay his owner many times over with companionship and unwavering devotion.

Show off your artistic side. Share photos, videos and artwork of your favorite breed on Club Chi. You can also submit jokes, riddles and even poetry about Chihuahuas. Browse through our various galleries and see the talent of fellow toy dog owners. Go to **DogChannel.com/Club-Chi** and click on "Galleries" to get started.

JOIN OUR ONLINE Club Chi™

NOTABLE & QUOTABLE

Life with an adult Chihuahua follows more of a routine than life with a puppy; but having a Chihuahua is like having a puppy for life. I still take my Chihuahuas everywhere with me. We still play hard and then cuddle. It amazes me how different their personalities are — how so much personality can fit into something so tiny. It's easier with adults, but every bit as wonderful!

— Ruth Link, Chi owner from Missoula, Mont.

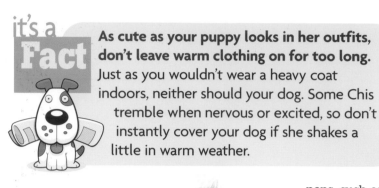

it's a **Fact**

As cute as your puppy looks in her outfits, don't leave warm clothing on for too long. Just as you wouldn't wear a heavy coat indoors, neither should your dog. Some Chis tremble when nervous or excited, so don't instantly cover your dog if she shakes a little in warm weather.

THE TREMBLES

You might have heard that Chihuahuas tend to be high-strung; they react readily to stimuli and will bark, jump around, spin in circles or perform other energy-releasing behaviors when something happens, such as the doorbell ringing.

If a Chihuahua can't release his energy for whatever reason, he is likely to become nervous and start shaking — what you might call a basic case of the jitters. "I see this kind of anxiety when an owner is holding their Chi and a stranger approaches," says longtime Chihuahua breeder Rita Geiger, of New Ulm, Minn.

Obviously, restraint prevents the Chi from releasing energy. Nervous energy partially explains why some dogs who are frequently carried exhibit aggression when a stranger comes near. Barking and growling serve as energy releases and cause what makes them nervous to go away.

However, not every Chihuahua gets the jitters, according to Shelly Covelli, a dog-show participant and Chi owner from Weldona, Colo.

"My male never shakes," Covelli says. "He takes things in stride. My female shakes when she is in any new situation."

Though some Chis display nervous tendencies, the best approach to help your puppy avoid becoming a jittery adult is through careful socialization and training to acclimate him to different environments. Just make sure you remember his sweater in chilly weather!

As cute as he looks in a designer handbag, your Chi can't spend his life glued to your side. Let him loose, so he can explore his world!

Pop Pups

Chis vs. Children

The trouble with Chihuahuas is that when it comes to children, they look an awful lot like something to play with. Although they are members of the Toy Group, Chihuahuas are not toys to amuse children. "I'm pretty leery about letting small children around Chihuahuas," says Sharon Hermosillo of San Jose, Calif., a Chihuahua breeder and former rescue chairperson of the Chihuahua Club of America. "I have three grandchildren, but I knew I had to teach them how to handle the dogs, not train the dogs how to handle the kids."

Although children, especially older children, can be taught how to handle a small dog without injuring her or risking a nip, some children simply don't have the patience. A toddler who is too young to control his or her behavior should never be trusted around a Chihuahua, and very high-energy kids may make a Chihuahua nervous, especially if your dog hasn't been exposed to children.

"I always keep a cautious eye on my Chihuahuas around children," says Chi owner Nancy Robbins of Suwanee, Ga. "My Chihuahuas tend to be nervous out in public, and they aren't used to children around the house, where they are most comfortable, except for my two daughters."

Even when she was younger, Robbins' 8-year-old daughter sometimes pushed her Chis to the limit. "When she pushed them too far, they would snap at her," Robbins explains. "They hadn't been around younger children and didn't like it when kids ran or got loud around them."

Of course, some Chis do very well around children, but much depends on the individual personality of your dog and, once again, whether she is exposed to children at a young age. "In my opinion, when it comes to Chihuahuas and children, there should always be close supervision," Robbins says.

If your family has small children, you may be better off waiting until they are older to bring home a Chihuahua. If you already own a Chihuahua when you have children, careful supervision is key at all times. Remember, Chihuahuas thrive on being the center of attention, so when a new baby joins the family, your Chi will need a lot of extra attention, support and love, so she will know you've got more than enough love for all the little creatures in your family.

Chis are lovable dogs who simply wish to spend their days playing and cuddling with their owners

A CHI CHART
The world's smallest dog has a big personality.

COUNTRY OF ORIGIN: Mexico

WHAT HIS FRIENDS CALL HIM: Chi, Tiny, Señor, Perro

SIZE: 6 to 9 inches tall at the shoulders, weighing 2 to 6 pounds

COAT & COLOR: Chihuahua's coats can come in two varieties: long or smooth. Long coats are soft, flat or slightly curly with an undercoat with a large ruff on the neck and feathering on the tail, feet and legs. Smooth coats are soft, glossy and have straight hair. Any color is permissible, but the most common are red, sable, fawn, black and tan, tricolor and brindle.

PERSONALITY TRAITS: These dogs are alert, sensitive and spirited. They are great companions, which makes them ideal for individuals.

WITH KIDS: Chihuahuas may not be great with children at first; they require socialization to be comfortable around them. Children also will need to be taught how to handle the dog appropriately.

WITH OTHER PETS: Chihuahuas work best with other Chis

ENERGY LEVEL: low

EXERCISE NEEDS: Their needs are not extensive: daily walks, playing and the occasional shopping trip.

GROOMING NEEDS: weekly brushing. Sometimes more grooming is needed for long-coat Chis.

TRAINING NEEDS: Chihuahuas are trainable, but be cautious of their delicate bodies when teaching them new things.

LIVING ENVIRONMENT: These toy dogs make great apartment companions, especially for an individual, or a sedentary or elderly adult.

LIFESPAN: Chihuahuas live well into their teen years.

CHAPTER 2

TOY DOG

TALES

The Chihuahua may be small, but he's not short on history. This miniature breed has a rich and colorful past. Although nobody thought to keep written accounts of the breed as it was developing centuries ago, modern historians can recreate its origins with some degree of accuracy.

Stone carvings, clay figures and mummified remains unearthed at archeological digs in Central America provide a framework from which breeders and fanciers enthusiastically conjecture the Chihuahua's history. Folklore and facts throughout this breed's history create several possibilities. Those competing theories will probably never be entirely settled, but if the Chihuahua were keeping his own oral history, it might go something like this …

ONCE UPON A TIME

The three major pre-Columbian civilizations — the Maya, the Toltec and the Aztec — all show evidence of a close association with a small, sandy-colored dog who is most likely the progenitor of the modern Chihuahua. The exact origins and genetic make up of these dogs are the subject of much hypothesis. These dogs mingled in various degrees with the Xoloitzcuintli, a small, hairless, local breed. The Xoloitzcuintli originated in Asia

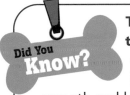

Did You Know? The Chihuahua is the world's smallest dog. The tiny breed comes in smooth and long-coat varieties.

The Chihuahua's batlike ears and apple-shaped head are breed trademarks.

and is suspected to be the forerunner of the Chinese Crested and other early canine varieties who moved to Central and South America via Mediterranean trade routes from the Middle East.

The earliest definitive evidence that an ancient dog resembling the Chihuahua existed was discovered at Toltecan archeological sites. The Toltec were an indigenous Mesoamerican people who established an extensive empire in the 10th century. They inhabited the land extending all the way from central North America to southern Mexico. Excavations of Toltec sites have unearthed canine remains of small dogs, which the Toltec called "Techichi."

The Toltec civilization was steeped in mysticism. They were a shamanistic culture and ascribed spiritual connotations to nearly every aspect of the natural world. It is likely that their small dogs held spiritual significance for them and may have played a role in their rituals.

The Toltec were also an aggressive people. As they migrated south from North America, they established new cities and conquered existing ones. Their dogs traveled with them, and eventually, the little

it's a Fact

Chis can be found in any color, from snow white to the darkest black. The color may be solid, covering the entire dog, or it may be marked or splashed. Markings are generally accepted as patches of color, such as tan eyebrows, cheek patches, patches on the feet, spots on the front of the chest and a circle under the tail of a black dog. Splashes refer to irregularly shaped spots of color on a white Chihuahua or white patches on a dog of color. Common splashes are saddles on the back and colored ears. In the United States, solid colors are more popular, with cream, tan and red seen most often. However, in Mexico, solid black and black-and-tan Chihuahuas are most commonly seen.

They may be little, but Chihuahuas have a rich and well-established history.

rust-colored Techichi was established over much of the subcontinent. Like the Maya whom they conquered, the Toltec tabulated their daily and seasonal activities in stone carvings, called "codices." Some of these codices depict a very small, big-eared dog who bears a striking resemblance to the Chihuahua of today.

In the 1500s, Franciscan monks used stones from a ruined Toltec temple to construct a monastery. The monastery, known as Huejotzingo, is located about 40 miles north of Mexico City. The carved images of small, big-eared dogs seen on these stones are some of the best examples of the Chihuahua's ancient beginnings. They depict an unmistakable body profile similar to the modern Chihuahua. These carvings, along with Mayan carvings and relics found in the Yucatan, are perhaps the most definitive proof that the Techichi is the progenitor of today's Chihuahua.

Just as the Toltec conquered the Maya, so did the Aztecs eventually conquer the Toltec. Survivors, both human and canine, were absorbed by the new culture. Aztec emperors and the ruling class revered their little dogs and kept them close in life and death.

The Aztec believed Techichis to be spiritual guides for the dead, and remains of small dogs similar to the Chihuahua have been unearthed at burial sites alongside human remains. The dogs were sacrificed

and interred with their master's remains with the belief that the sins of the master would be transferred to the dog, thus ensuring the master's safe passage to his spiritual resting place.

The breed flourished in Mexico during the reign of Montezuma, the last of the great Aztec emperors. The ruler is known to have

Did You Know? For years, Chihuahua fanciers strove to organize a club, but dissension over the standard — particularly the tail — caused the postponement of establishing a breed club until Feb. 1, 1923. The cycle tail was agreed upon as a happy medium between the so-called 'rat-tail' and the flat, furry tail. The cycle tail is carried in a small loop over the back and covered by close, dense hair. It is still described in the Chihuahua breed standard today.

You have an unbreakable bond with your dog, but do you always understand him? Go online and download "Dog Speak," which outlines how dogs communicate. Find out what your Chihuahua is saying when he barks, howls or growls. Go to **DogChannel.com/Club-Chi** and click on "Downloads."

JOIN OUR ONLINE **Club Chi**™

SMART TIP!

Chihuahuas tend to do very well with other dogs of their own kind. If you are concerned about not giving your Chi enough attention, consider getting another Chihuahua so they can play together.

been quite a fancier of the Techichi, and it is likely that he was responsible for their introduction into northern Mexico, the modern-day state of Chihuahua.

COMING TO AMERICA

In 1520, Spanish explorer Hernando Cortez and his armies conquered the Aztec empire, and the little dogs with the big ears were nearly wiped out. Far from receiving the royal treatment lavished upon them by the Aztecs, the Chihuahua became a food source for the Spaniards.

A few of the dogs found refuge with peasant families, and many escaped into the wild. A feral dog known as *perro chi-huahuaeno* still inhabits the mountainous regions of the northernmost state of Chihuahua; these dogs exhibit varying degrees of Chi characteristics. Specimens on exhibit at the National Museum of Natural History in Mexico City show three distinct individuals. One is a fawn-colored dog weighing about 3 pounds, with a roached back, weak legs and a fairly good Chihuahua-type head. Another is a tricolored dog weighing about 7 pounds. The third canine specimen is fawn in color, weighing about 3½ pounds, with a classic "apple dome" skull cherished by Chihuahua breeders today.

True Tails

Beyond the Call of Duty

Nacho, a Chihuahua mix, joined the Hounsell family of Hood River, Ore., in January 1984 to serve as a hearing assistance dog to Betty, 62, and her husband, John, 72. Nacho was meant primarily to aid Betty, who had lost about 95 percent of her hearing over a few short years. But John's hearing also wasn't as acute as it used to be, so the couple began to rely on Nacho.

Trained by Dogs for the Deaf in Central Point, Ore., Nacho alerted the Hounsells to a variety of sounds, including the doorbell, the telephone, oven buzzers and fire alarms, by placing her paw on the couple and leading them to the source of the sound. On Feb. 25, 1985, barely 13 months after joining the Hounsell family, Nacho alerted the Hounsells for one last time.

Upon hearing an unusual noise in the otherwise quiet home, Nacho began barking and frantically awakened the couple with a touch of her paw. At this point, accounts vary about whether the Hounsells left their bedroom in search of the noise or if events transpired too quickly for action. The noise Nacho heard was made by what John thought to be three intruders. Before fleeing with $80, identification materials, a checkbook and credit cards, one of the burglars slashed Nacho's throat with a hunting knife.

In the Feb. 27, 1985, edition of the *Hood River News*, it was reported that investigators found the couple's telephone wires had been ripped from the wall and that the burglars had entered the home through a broken basement window. The local police credited Nacho with "probably saving the Hounsells' lives and certainly preventing serious injury."

That May, nearly three months following her death, Nacho was honored with the American Humane Association's William O. Stillman Award for Bravery. The award, first bestowed in 1900, goes to animals who have saved human lives in the face of danger and to humans who have put themselves at great risk to rescue animals.

Did You Know? The Chihuahua breed standard, the written description of the perfect Chi, states that these dogs are not to exceed 6 pounds. That is the only size description allowed. The Chihuahua Club of America does not recognize: teacup, pocket, tiny toys, miniatures, baby dolls or any other labels. These misleading terms are used by unscrupulous breeders to scam potential owners out of money.

Interestingly, in the mid-1600s, small, smooth-coated dogs with *moleras* — also known as an "open fontanel" or "hole in the head" (like a human infant), one of the breed's most distinctive characteristics — appeared in Europe. Dogs with Chi features gained favor with the upper class and can be found in classical paintings of the time. It is possible that some of the Techichi made their way back to Spain during the colonization period which followed the conquest. Other reports suggest these dogs originated in Egypt and made their way to Europe via Malta.

By the mid-1800s, the tiny dogs with the conspicuously huge ears had recovered from the perils of Mexico's war for independence and could be found throughout Mexico. In 1850, some American tourists purchased two pair from the state of Chihuahua and brought them home. In the United States, these peculiar little dogs were immediately named "Mexican Chihuahuas."

His small size, distinct face and affectionate nature made the Chi an ideal companion dog, but it took several decades of dedicated breeding before the Chihuahua could endear himself to the American public. The first men-

tion of the breed in the American Kennel Club stud book is found in the 1890 edition, which notes the wins of four unregistered dogs: Anno, Bob, Eyah and Pepity.

The Chihuahua Club of America was founded in 1923. With the formation of a national club and the acceptance of the standard, breeding took on a more focused approach. The club's first national specialty was held in 1928, on Geraldine Rockefeller Dodge's New Jersey estate. The gracious estate was the site for the annual Morris and Essex Show, the most prestigious dog show in the country at that time.

The addition of the national specialty was made possible by a generous donation from Henrietta Procter Darnell, heiress to the Procter & Gamble fortune. Darnell did not own Chihuahuas but was asked to be the president of the national club specifically to gain her financial support. Dogs and owners arrived by train at a private station located on the property. Waiters in white coats glided between tents carrying trays of champagne and caviar, and dogs competed for solid silver trophies. Seeing the scrappy little dogs in such distinguished company, those early breeders must have felt as though they

JOIN OUR ONLINE Club Chi™

Just how quickly will your Chihuahua puppy grow?
Go to Club Chi and download a growth chart. You also can see your pup's age in human years; the old standard of multiplying your dog's age by seven isn't quite accurate. Log onto **DogChannel.com/Club-Chi** and click on "Downloads."

Being popular isn't always a good thing. Chis, unfortunately, are often bred by puppy millers in unfit conditions solely for profit. Be aware, and purchase your puppy from a responsible breeder.

had finally arrived; the future of the breed seemed assured.

In 1950, there was a sudden surge in popularity that may have been related to post-World War I settlement patterns. More Americans were moving into the cities and becoming apartment dwellers and suburban homeowners after the war. Toy dogs as a group came into their own, and during the '50s, the Chihuahua became the most popular dog in the country.

Since that rapid rise to fame, the Chi has consistently ranked among the top 15 of all AKC registered breeds. In the 1990s, there was another surge in popularity, which can be explained in two words: Taco Bell.

NOTABLE & QUOTABLE

There is always a shortage of quality dogs, compared to demand. Chihuahuas do not have large litters, and there is a high mortality rate among puppies. They are very fragile for the first few weeks of their lives.

— B. J. Shears, a Chihuahua breeder from Altamont, Kan.

Much to the horror and chagrin of serious fanciers, the Mexican-style fast-food chain chose a Chihuahua for its media mascot; but not just any Chihuahua — a really poor example of the standard, saying and doing irresistibly cute things in adorable outfits. Predictably, the American public ate it up. The advertising campaign spawned a sudden demand for dogs who looked like the Taco Bell dog.

Spikes in the marketplace can cause thoughtful breeding to go by the wayside. Backyard breeders were suddenly motivated to breed Chihuahuas because they knew there was a demand for puppies; fad dog buyers are less likely to educate themselves about the particular requirements and limitations of the breed.

Just as Dalmatian breeders had to battle the breed's surge in popularity in the wake of Disney's *101 Dalmatians* (1961), so too did responsible Chihuahua breeders struggle to keep from losing the ground they had gained from years of careful, selective breeding. Breed rescues were on alert for an expected influx of abandoned dogs who didn't meet the needs of the people who bought them.

But the future of the Chihuahua breed is now in good hands. Dedicated, responsible breeders are in it for the love of the breed and sincerely want to see the breed strengthen and improve. Research and education regarding genetic defects is being put to good use.

As Chihuahua breeders and judges become more informed, their decisions are yielding a better quality of show champions than at any other time in the breed's history. For a dog who was once valued as a main dish, the challenge of managing his burgeoning popularity seems like a happy problem indeed!

Long-coat Chihuahuas are genetically the same as their smooth counterparts, albeit with more and longer hair.

SELECTION

Tracking down either a smooth or a long-coat Chihuahua puppy from a dedicated, conscientious breeder is the first step in your search for a new dog. If you don't know anyone who can refer you to a quality breeder, figuring out where to look for one can be a challenge. According to the American Kennel Club, which maintains a registry of purebreds and tabulates how many litters and dogs in each breed are registered every year, the Chihuahua is consistently one of the top 15 most popular breeds. This means there's no shortage of breeders who sell puppies. In fact, you can pretty much find Chihuahua pups for sale everywhere you look. However, finding a quality breeder who has a perfect and healthy Chihuahua for you requires a little detective work and some patience, but the search is well worth the effort.

You're going to have your Chihuahua well into his teens, so the time you spend early on to locate a healthy, well-adjusted puppy from a reputable breeder will pay off for you

it's a Fact

Have your Chi examined by a veterinarian within two to three days after purchasing. If declared unhealthy, the breeder should take the dog back without any problems, which shows confidence and that the breeder stands behind his or her dogs. The willingness to rehome a puppy is the ultimate hallmark of a good breeder.

in the long run. Look for a dedicated and ethical breeder who values good health and stable personalities, and one who really cares what happens to the dog for the rest of his life spent with you.

Be sure to avoid puppy mills and backyard breeders. Puppy mills are large-scale breeding operations that produce puppies in an assembly-line fashion without regard to health and socialization. Backyard breeders are typically well-meaning pet owners who simply do not possess enough knowledge about their breed and breeding to produce healthy puppies.

The American Kennel Club (www.akc.org) and United Kennel Club (www.ukcdogs.com) provide lists of breeders in good standing with their organizations. Visit their websites for more information.

EVALUATING BREEDERS

Once you have the names and numbers of breeders in your area, start contacting them to find out more about their breeding programs. Before you pick up the phone, prepare a list of questions that will get you the information you need to know.

Prospective buyers should interview breeders much the same way that a breeder interviews a buyer. Make a list of questions and record the answers so you can compare them to the answers from other breeders

whom you may interview later. The right questions are those that help you identify who has been in the breed a respectable number of years and who is actively showing their dogs. Ask in-depth questions regarding the genetic health of the parents, grandparents and great-grandparents of any puppy you are considering. Ask what sort of genetic testing program the breeder adheres to.

A prospective buyer should look to see if a breeder actively shows his or her dogs. Showing indicates that the breeder is bringing out examples from his or her breeding program for the public to see. If there are any obvious problems, such as temperament or general conformation, they will be readily apparent. Also, the main reason to breed dogs is to improve the quality of the breed. If the breeder is not showing, then he or she is more likely breeding for the monetary aspect and may have less concern for the welfare and future of the breed.

Smart potential puppy buyers inquire about health and determine the breeder's willingness to work with them in the future. The prospective buyer should see what kind of health guarantees the breeder gives. You should also find out if the breeder will be available for future consultation regarding your dog, and find out if the breeder will take him back if something unforeseen happens.

Prospective buyers should ask plenty of questions, and in return, they should be prepared to answer questions posed by a responsible breeder who wants to make sure their Chi puppy is going to a good home. Be prepared for a battery of questions from the breeder regarding your purpose for wanting a Chihuahua and whether or not you can properly care for one. Avoid buying from a breeder who does little or no screening. If

Did You Know?

When you visit a Chihuahua breeder, be sure to look around the location for:
- a clean, well-maintained facility
- no overwhelming odors
- overall impression of cleanliness
- socialized dogs and puppies

If someone says they're selling a "teacup," "miniature" or "pocket" Chihuahua puppy who will weigh 1 to 2 pounds when fully grown, don't believe them. This is just an advertising buzz word to trick unsuspecting buyers.
— *Chihuahua breeder and American Kennel Club judge Michael Heflin*

breeders don't ask questions, they are not concerned with where their toy puppies end up. In this case, the dogs' best interests are probably not the breeder's motive for breeding. You should find a breeder who is willing to answer any questions you have and is knowledgeable about the history of the breed, health issues and about the background of their own dogs. Learn about a breeder's long-term commitment to the breed and to their puppies after they leave the kennel.

Look for a breeder who knows their purpose for producing a particular litter, one who is knowledgeable of the pedigrees of their dogs and of the breed itself and has had the necessary health screenings performed on the parents. The breeder should also be asking you for references if they are interested in establishing a relationship with you. If after one phone conversation with a breeder, they supply you with an address to send a deposit, continue your search for a reputable breeder elsewhere.

CHOOSING THE RIGHT PUP

Once you have found a breeder you are comfortable with, your next step is to pick the right puppy for you. The good news is that if you have done your homework in finding a responsible breeder, you can count on this person to give you plenty of help in choosing the right pup for your personality and lifestyle. In fact, most good breeders will recommend a specific puppy to a buyer once they know what kind of dog the buyer wants.

After you have narrowed down the search and selected a reputable breeder, rely on the experience of the breeder to help you select the exact puppy. The selection of the puppy depends a lot on what purpose the pup is being purchased for. If the pup is being purchased as a show prospect, the breeder will offer their assessment of the pups who meet this criteria and be able to explain the strengths and faults of each pup.

Whether your pup is show- or pet-quality, a good, stable temperament is vital for a happy relationship. Generally, you want to avoid a timid puppy or one who is very dominant. Temperament is very important, and a reputable breeder should spend a lot of time with the pups and be able to offer an evaluation of each pup's personality.

Reputable breeders should tell each buyer which puppy is appropriate for their home situation and personalities. They may not allow you to choose the puppy, although they will certainly take your preference into consideration. Some breeders, on the other hand, believe it's important for you to have a strong involvement in picking a puppy from the litter. Not everyone is looking for the same things in a dog. Some people want a

quiet, laidback attitude. Others want an outgoing, active dog.

When pups are old enough to go to their new homes at roughly 10 to 12 weeks of age, some breeders prefer that you make your own decision because no one can tell at this age which pup will make the most intelligent or affectionate dog. The color, sex and markings are obvious, but that is about all you can tell for sure at this age. Everything else being equal — size, health, etc. — you might just pick the pup who you have a gut feeling for.

Chemistry between the buyer and a puppy is important and should play a role in determining which pup goes to which home. When possible, make numerous visits, and in effect, let a puppy choose you. There usually will be one puppy who spends more time with a buyer and is more comfortable relaxing and sitting with or on them. This is a sign that you have finally found your Chi pup.

JOIN OUR ONLINE
Club Chi™

Questions to Expect
Be prepared for the breeder to ask you some questions, too.

This isn't a steadfast rule, and some breeders insist on meeting the children to see how they handle puppies; it all depends on the breeder.

1. Have you previously owned a Chihuahua?
The breeder is trying to gauge how familiar you are with the breed. If you have never owned one, illustrate your knowledge of Chihuahuas by telling the breeder about your research.

2. Do you have children? What are their ages?
Some breeders are wary about selling a dog to families with younger children.

3. How long have you wanted a Chihuahua?
This helps a breeder know if this purchase is an impulse buy or a carefully thought-out decision. Buying on impulse is one of the biggest mistakes owners can make. Be patient.

Join Club Chi to get a complete list of questions a breeder should ask you. Click on "Downloads" at: **DogChannel.com/Club-Chi**

CHECKING FOR CHI QUALITIES

Whether you are dealing with a breeder who wants to pick a pup for you or lets you make the decision alone, consider certain points when evaluating the pup you may end up calling your own. The pup should be friendly and outgoing, not skittish in any way. He should be forgiving of correction. He shouldn't be too terribly mouthy. The pup should readily follow you and be willing to snuggle in your lap and be turned onto his back easily without a problem.

Proper temperament is important. A Chihuahua puppy who has a dominant personality requires an experienced owner who will be firm during training. A puppy who is a little shy will require heavy socialization to build his confidence.

Evaluate each puppy's temperament on your own, with the breeder's permission. The temperament of the pups can be evaluated by spending some time watching them. If you can visit the pups and observe them together with their littermates, you can see how they interact with each other. You may be able to pinpoint which ones are the bullies and which ones are more submissive. In general, look for a puppy who is more interested in you than his littermates. Then, take each pup individually to a new location away from the rest of the litter. Put the pup down on the ground, walk away and see

With the popularity of Chihuahuas, shelters and rescue groups across the country are often inundated with sweet, loving examples of the breed — from the tiniest puppies to senior dogs.

Often, to get the Chihuahua of your dreams, it only takes a journey to the local shelter. Or, perhaps you could find your ideal dog waiting patiently in the arms of a foster parent at a nearby rescue group. It just takes a bit of effort, patience and a willingness to find the right dog for your family — not just the cutest dog on the block.

The perks of owning a Chihuahua are plentiful: companionship, unconditional love, true loyalty and laughter, just to name a few. So why choose the adoption option? Because you literally will be saving a life!

Owners of adopted dogs swear they're more grateful and loving than any dog they've owned before. It's almost as if they knew what dire fate awaited them and are so thankful to you. Chihuahuas, known for their people-pleasing personalities, seem to embody this mentality whole-heartedly when they're rescued. And they want to give something back to the owners who saved them.

Another perk: Almost all adopted dogs come fully vetted, with proper medical treatment, vaccinations, medicine, as well as being spayed or neutered. Some are even licensed and microchipped.

Don't disregard older dogs, thinking the only good pair-up is you and a puppy. Adult Chis are more established behaviorally and personality-wise, helping to better mesh their characteristics with yours in this game of matchmaker. Pups are always in high demand, so if you open your options to include adult dogs in your search, you'll have a better chance of adopting quickly. Plus, adult dogs are often housetrained, more calm and don't need to be taken outside in the middle of the night ... five times .. in the pouring rain.

The Chihuahua Club of America offers rescue support information (www.chihuahuaclubofamerica.com) or log onto Petfinder.com (www.petfinder.com). The site's searchable database enables you to find a Chi puppy in your area who needs a break in the form of a smart owner like you. More websites are listed in the Resources chapter on page 166.

how he reacts away from the security of his littermates. The pup may be afraid at first, but should gradually recover and start checking out the new surroundings

D-I-Y TEMPERAMENT TEST

Puppies come in a wide assortment of temperaments to suit just about everyone. If you are looking for a Chihuahua who is easily trainable and a good companion to your family, you most likely want a dog with a medium temperament.

Temperament testing can help you determine the type of disposition your potential puppy possesses. A pup with a medium, trainable temperament will have the following reactions to these various tests, best conducted when the pup is about 7 weeks.

Step 1. To test a Chi pup's social attraction to humans and his confidence or shyness in approaching them, coax him toward you by kneeling down and clapping your hands gently. A puppy with a medium temperament will come readily, tail up or down.

Step 2. To test a pup's eagerness to follow you, walk away from him while he is watching you. The pup should readily follow you with his tail up.

Step 3. To see how a Chi pup handles restraint, kneel down and roll the pup gently on his back. Using a light but firm touch, hold him in this position with one hand for 30 seconds. The pup should settle down after some initial struggle and offer some, or steady, eye contact.

Step 4. To evaluate a pup's level of social dominance, stand up, then crouch down beside the pup and stroke him from head to tail. A pup with a medium temperament, neither too dominant nor too submissive, should cuddle up to you and lick your face or squirm and lick your hands.

Step 5. An additional test of a pup's dominance is to bend over, cradle him under his belly with your fingers interlaced, palms up, and elevate him just off the ground. Hold for 30 seconds. He should not struggle and should be relaxed, or he should struggle and then settle down and lick you.

A HEALTHY PUPPY

To assess a puppy's health, take a deliberate, thorough look at each part of his body. A healthy puppy has bright eyes, a healthy coat, a good appetite and firm stool.

Watch for a telltale link between physical and mental health. A healthy Chihuahua, as with any breed of puppy, will display a happier, more positive attitude than an unhealthy puppy. A pup's belly should not be over extended or hard, as this may be a sign of worms. Also, if you are around the litter long enough to witness a bowel movement, the stool should be solid, and the pup should not show any signs of discomfort. Look into the pup's eyes, too, they should be bright and full of life.

When purchasing a Chihuahua puppy, buyers hear from breeders that these dogs

Did You Know? Properly bred puppies come from parents who were selected based upon their genetic disease profile. Their mothers should be vaccinated, free of all internal and external parasites, and properly nourished. For these reasons, a visit to the veterinarian who cared for the mother is recommended. The mother can pass on disease resistance to her puppies, which can last for 8 to 10 weeks.

Breeder Q&A
Here are some questions *you* should ask a breeder and the answers you want.

Q. How often do you have litters available?
A. The answer you want to hear is "occasionally" or "once or twice a year." A breeder who doesn't have litters all that often is probably more concerned with the quality of his puppies, rather than making money.

Q. What kinds of health issues have you had with your Chihuahua?
A. Beware of a breeder who says, "none." Every breed has health issues. For Chis, some health problems include hypoglycemia, hip dysplasia, heartworms and tracheal collapse.

Get a complete list of questions that you can ask a Chihuahua breeder — and the correct answers they should give — on Club Chi. Log onto **DogChannel.com/Club-Chi** and click on "Downloads."

it's a **Fact**

Food intolerance is the inability of the dog to completely digest certain foods. Puppies who have done very well on their mother's milk may not do well on cow's milk. The result of this food intolerance may be loose bowels, passing gas and stomach pains. These are the only obvious symptoms of food intolerance, which makes diagnosis difficult.

are just like any other puppy — times 10! They are very smart, calculating, stubborn and often have their own agendas. If prospective owners aren't willing to spend a fair amount of time with a Chihuahua, then the breed is not for them. This toy breed wants to be with people more than most dogs and is quite like a 7-year-old boy in that he needs attention and consistent positive reinforcement for good behaviors. Once through adolescence, however, a Chihuahua is the best friend, house alarm and companion a person or family could have.

PUPPY PARTICULARS

Here are signs to look for when picking a Chi puppy from a breeder. When in doubt, ask the breeder which puppy they think has the best personality and temperament to fit your lifestyle.

1. Look at the area where the pups spend most of their time. It is OK if they play outdoors part of the day, but they should sleep indoors at night so the pups can interact with people and become accustomed to hearing ordinary household noises. This builds a solid foundation for a secure, well-socialized puppy. The puppy area should be clean, well-lit, have fresh drinking water and interesting toys.

2. Sure, you're only buying one puppy, but make sure to see all of the puppies in the litter. By 5 weeks of age, healthy pups will begin playing with one another and should be lively and energetic. It's OK if they're asleep when you visit, but stay long enough to see them wake up. Once they're up, they shouldn't be lethargic or weak.

3. Pups should be confident and eager to greet you. A pup who is shy or fearful

A smart, potential Chi owner will visit the breeder several times to observe the puppies and get a sense of the litter's overall well-being.

and stays in the corner may be sick or insecure. Although some introverted pups come out of their shells later on, many do not. These dogs will be fearful as adults and are not good choices for an active, noisy family (with or without children) or for people who have never had a dog. These dogs frighten easily and will require a tremendous amount of training and socialization.

Choose a pup who is happy and eager to interact with you but reject the one who is either too shy or too bossy. These temperament types are a challenge to deal with, and require a lot of training to socialize. The perfect Chihuahua puppy personality is somewhere between the two extremes.

4. If it's feeding time during your visit, all pups should be eager to gobble up their food. Refusing to eat may signal illness.

5. The dog's skin should be smooth, clean and shiny without any sores or bumps. Puppies should not be biting or scratching at themselves continuously, which could be a sign of fleas.

6. After 10 to 12 days, their eyes should be open and clear without any redness or discharge. Pups should not scratch at their eyes, this may cause an infection or signal irritation.

7. Vomiting or coughing more than once is not normal. The pup may be ill and should visit the veterinarian.

8. Visit long enough to see the pups eliminate. All stools should be firm without being watery or bloody. These are signs of illness or that a puppy has worms.

9. Chihuahua puppies should walk or run without limping.

10. A healthy puppy who eats enough should not be skinny. You should be able to slightly feel his ribs, but you should not be able to see them.

BREEDER PAPERS

Everything today comes with an instruction manual. When you purchase a Chihuahua, it's no different. A reputable breeder should give you a registration application, a sales contract, a health guarantee, the dog's complete health records, a three-, four- or five-generation pedigree and some general information about behavior, care, conformation, health and training.

Registration Application. This document from the AKC, UKC or American Dog Breeders Association assigns your puppy a number and identifies the dog by listing his date of birth, the names of the parents and shows that he is registered as a purebred Chihuahua. It doesn't prove whether or not your dog is a show- or a pet-quality Chi and doesn't provide any health guarantee.

Sales Contract. Reputable breeders discuss the terms of the contract before asking you to sign it. This is a written understanding of your expectations about the puppy and shows that the breeder cares about the puppy's welfare throughout his life. The contract can include such terms as requiring you to keep your dog indoors at night, spaying or neutering if your puppy is not going to be a show dog, providing routine veterinary care throughout your dog's life, and assurance that you'll feed your dog a healthy diet. Most responsible dog breeders will ask that you take your dog to obedience classes and earn a Canine Good Citizen title on him before 2 years of age. Many breeders also require new owners to have totally secure fencing and gates around their yard. Chihuahuas can be incredible escape artists, and they will find a way out of the yard if there's even the slightest opening.

Health Guarantee. This includes a letter from a veterinarian that the puppy has been examined and is healthy, and states that the breeder will replace the dog if the pup develops a genetic, life-threatening illness during his lifetime.

Health Records. This is everything you want to know about not only your puppy's health but also the parents' as well.

It should include the dates the puppy was vaccinated, dewormed and examined by a veterinarian for signs of a heart murmur, plus the parents' test results for the presence or absence of hip and elbow dysplasia, heart problems and slipped patellas.

Pedigree. Breeders should give you a copy of your Chi puppy's three-, four- or five-generation pedigree. Many have photos of your dog's ancestors they will proudly share with you.

Information. The best breeders pride themselves on handing over a notebook full of the latest information on Chihuahua behavior, care, conformation, health and training. Be sure to read it because it will provide invaluable help while raising your Chihuahua.

Signs of a Healthy Puppy
Here are a few things you should look for when selecting a puppy from a litter.

1. **NOSE:** It should be slightly moist to the touch but there shouldn't be excessive discharge. The puppy should not be sneezing or persistently sniffling.

2. **SKIN AND COAT:** A Chi puppy's coat should be soft and shiny, without flakes or excessive shedding. Watch out for patches of missing hair, redness, bumps or sores. The pup should have a pleasant smell. Check for parasites, such as fleas or ticks.

3. **BEHAVIOR:** A healthy Chihuahua puppy may be sleepy but he should not be lethargic. A healthy pup will be playful at times, not isolated in a corner. You should see occasional bursts of energy and interaction with littermates. When it's mealtime, a healthy pup will take an interest in his food.

There are more signs to look for when picking out the perfect Chihuahua puppy for you. Download the list at **DogChannel.com/Club-Chi**

CHAPTER 4

HOME

ESSENTIALS

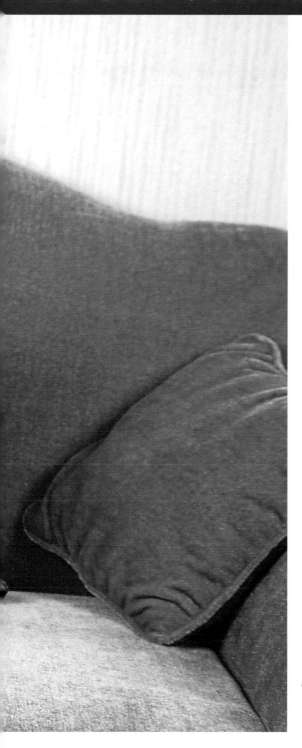

Don't think for one second that a toy dog would prefer to live in a place described as a box or pen. He, like every other breed, wants to live with the best accommodations such as plenty of toys, soft bedding and other luxuries. Your home is now his home, too. Before you bring that new Chi puppy or rescue dog into his new forever home, you need to make it accessible and comfortable for him.

In fact, in order for him to grow into a stable, well-adjusted Chihuahua, he has to feel comfortable in his surroundings. Remember, he is leaving the warmth and security of his mother and littermates, as well as the familiarity of the only place he has ever known, so it is important to make his transition to your home — his new home — as easy as possible.

PUPPY-PROOFING

Aside from making sure your Chihuahua will be comfortable in your home, you also have to ensure that your home is safe, which means taking the proper precautions to keep your pup away from things that are dangerous for him.

it's a Fact

Dangers lurk indoors and outdoors. Keep your curious Chihuahua from investigating your shed and garage. Antifreeze and fertilizers, such as those you would use for roses, will kill a dog. Keep these items on high shelves that are out of your dog's reach.

SMART TIP!

A well-stocked toy box should contain three main categories of toys:
1. **action** — anything that you can throw or roll and get things moving
2. **distraction** — durable toys that make dogs work for a treat
3. **comfort** — soft, stuffed little "security blankets"

A smart owner will puppy-proof their home inside and out before bringing their Chihuahua home for the first time. Place breakables out of reach. If he is limited to certain places within the house, keep potentially dangerous items in off-limit areas. If your Chihuahua is going to spend time in a crate, make sure that there is nothing near it he can reach if he sticks his curious little nose or paws through the openings.

The outside of your home must also be safe. Your puppy will want to run and explore the yard, and he should be granted that freedom — as long as you are there to supervise him. Do not let a fence give you a false sense of security; you would be surprised how crafty (and persistent) a dog can be in figuring out how to dig under a fence or squeeze his way through small holes. The remedy is to make the fence embedded into the ground. Be sure to repair or secure any gaps in the fence. A small dog, like your Chihuahua, can fit through the smallest hole. Check the fence periodically to ensure that it is in good shape and make repairs as needed; a very determined toy dog pup may work on the same spot until he is able to get through.

Smart owners will watch out for the following common problems in their homes:

■ **Electrical cords and wiring:** No electrical cord or wiring is safe. Many office-supply stores sell products to keep wires gathered under desks, as well as products that prevent chair wheels — and puppy teeth — from damaging electrical cords. If you have exposed cords and wires, these products aren't very expensive and can be used to keep a pup out of trouble.

■ **Trash cans:** Don't waste your time trying to train your Chi not to get into the trash. Dogs love bathroom trash (i.e., cotton balls, cotton swabs, dental floss, etc.), all of which are extremely dangerous! Simply put the garbage behind a cabinet door, using a child-safe lock, if necessary; and make sure you always shut the bathroom door.

■ **Household cleaners:** Make sure your Chihuahua puppy doesn't have access to any of these deadly chemicals. Keep them

behind closed cabinet doors, using child-safe locks if necessary.

■ **Pest control sprays and poisons:** Chemicals to control ants or other pests should not be used in the house, if possible. Your pup doesn't have to directly ingest these poisons to become ill; if your toy dog steps in the poison, he can experience toxic side effects from licking toxins off his paws. Roach motels and other poisonous pest traps can also be attractive to dogs, so do not drop these behind couches or cabinets; if there's room for a roach motel, there's room for a determined Chihuahua.

■ **Fabric:** Here's one you might not think about; some puppies have a habit of licking blankets, upholstery, rugs or carpets. Though this habit seems fairly innocuous, over time

the fibers from the upholstery or carpet can accumulate in the dog's stomach and cause a blockage. If you see your dog licking these items, remove the item or prevent him from having contact with it and give him something more suitable to sink his teeth into.

Did You Know? Some dog trainers recommend chewing deterrents, such as hot pepper or a product designed to discourage the dog from chewing on unwanted objects. This is sometimes reliable. Test out the product with your own dog before investing in a case of it.

■ **Prescriptions, painkillers, supplements and vitamins:** Keep all of your medications in a cabinet. Also, be very careful when taking your prescription medications, supplements or vitamins. How often have you dropped a pill? With a Chihuahua, you can be sure that your puppy will be at your feet and will snarf up the pill before you can even start to say "No!" Dispense your own pills carefully and without your Chihuahua present.

■ **Miscellaneous loose items:** If it's not bolted to the floor, your puppy is likely to give the item a taste test. Socks, coins, children's toys, game pieces, cat bell balls — you name it; if it's on the floor, it's worth a taste. Make sure the floors in your home are picked up and free of clutter.

JOIN OUR ONLINE **Club Chi™**

Before you bring your Chihuahua home, make sure you don't have anything that can put her in harm's way. Go to Club Chi and click "Downloads" for a list of poisonous plants and foods to avoid as well as a puppy-proofing checklist: **DogChannel.com/Club-Chi**

Make sure your house is ready for your new roommate. Keep hazardous items out of reach.

FAMILY INTRODUCTIONS

Everyone in the house will be excited about the puppy's homecoming and will want to pet and play with him, but it is best to make the introduction low-key so as not to overwhelm the puppy. He will already be apprehensive. It is the first time he has been separated from his mother, littermates and the breeder, and the ride to your home is likely to be the first time he has been in a car.

The last thing you want to do is smother your Chihuahua, as this will only frighten him further. This is not to say that human

NOTABLE & QUOTABLE

The first thing you should always do before your puppy comes home is to lie on the ground and look around. You want to be able to see everything your puppy is going to see. For the puppy, the world is one big chew toy.

— Cathleen Stamm, rescue volunteer in San Diego, Calif.

contact is not extremely necessary at this stage, this is the time when a connection between the pup and his human family is formed. Gentle petting and soothing words should help console your Chihuahua, as well as just putting him down and letting him explore on his own (under your watchful eye, of course).

Your dog may approach your family members or busy himself with exploring for a while. Gradually, each person should spend some time with the pup, one at a time, crouching down to get as close to the Chihuahua's level as possible and letting him sniff their hands before petting him gently. He definitely needs human attention and he needs to be touched; this is how to form an immediate bond. Just remember

that your pup is experiencing a lot of things for the first time, at the same time. There are new people, noises, smells and things to investigate, so be gentle, be affectionate and be as comforting as possible.

PUP'S FIRST NIGHT HOME

You have traveled home with your new charge safely in his crate. He may have already been to the vet for a thorough check-up — he's been weighed, his papers examined, perhaps he's even been vaccinated and dewormed. Your Chihuahua has met the whole family, including the excited children and the less-than-happy cat. He's explored his area, his new bed, the yard and anywhere else he's permitted. He's eaten his first meal at home and relieved himself in the proper place. Your Chihuahua has heard lots of new sounds, smelled new friends and seen more of the outside world than ever before.

This was just the first day! He's worn out and is ready for bed — or so you think!

Cratetraining is an invaluable housetraining tool for you and your Chihuahua

Remember, this is your puppy's first night to sleep alone. His mother and littermates are no longer at paw's length and he's scared, cold and lonely. Be reassuring to your new family member, but this is not the time to spoil your Chihuahua and give in to his inevitable whining.

Puppies whine. They whine to let others know where they are and hopefully to get company out of it. Place your Chihuahua puppy in his new bed or crate in his room and close the door. Mercifully, he may fall asleep without a peep. If the inevitable occurs, ignore the whining; he is fine. Do not give in and visit your puppy. Don't worry; he will fall asleep eventually.

Many breeders recommend placing a piece of bedding from a puppy's former home in his new bed so that he will recognize the scent of his littermates. Others advise placing a warm water bottle in his bed for warmth. The latter may be a good idea provided the pup doesn't attempt to suckle; he'll get good and wet and may not fall asleep so fast.

Your Chihuahua's first night in his new home can be somewhat terrifying for him. Remember, you set the tone of nighttime at your house. Unless you want to play with your pup every night at 10 p.m., midnight and 2 a.m., don't initiate the habit — even if your Chi is whining. Your family will thank you, and so will your pup!

SHOPPING FOR A CHIHUAHUA

It's fun shopping for a new puppy or rescue dog. From training to feeding and sleeping to playing, your new toy dog will need a few items to make life comfy, easy and fun. Be prepared and visit your local pet-supply store before you bring home your new family member.

◆ **Collar and ID tag:** Accustom your dog to wearing a collar the first day you bring him home. Not only will a collar and ID tag help your pup in the event that he becomes lost, collars will also be a handy training tool. If your toy dog gets into trouble, the collar will act as a handle, helping you divert him to a more appropriate behavior. Make sure the collar fits snugly enough so your Chi cannot wriggle out of it but is loose enough so it will not be uncomfortably tight around

his neck. You should be able to fit a finger between the pup and the collar. Collars come in many styles, but for starting out, a simple buckle collar with an easy-release snap works great.

◆ **Leash:** For training or just for taking a stroll down the street, a leash is your toy dog's means to explore the outside world. Like collars, leashes come in a variety of styles and materials. A 6-foot nylon leash is a popular choice because it is lightweight and durable. As your pup grows and gets used to walking on the leash, you may want to purchase a more flexible leash. These allow you to extend the length to give your dog a broader area to explore or to shorten the length to keep your dog closer to you.

◆ **Bowls:** Your toy dog will need two bowls — one for water and one for food. You may want two sets of bowls, one for inside and one for outside, depending on where your Chi will be fed and where he will be spending time. Bowls should be sturdy enough so they don't tip over easily. (Most have reinforced bottoms that prevent tipping.) Bowls usually are made of metal, ceramic or plastic and should be easy to clean.

◆ **Crate:** A multipurpose crate serves as a bed, house-training tool and travel

Nothing says home like a comfy doggie bed. Choose one that has durable lining so your teething puppy won't chew through it.

carrier. It also is the ideal doggie den — a bedroom of sorts — that your toy dog can retire to when he wants to rest or just needs a break. The crate should be large enough for your toy dog to stand in, turn around and lie down. You don't want any more room than this — especially if you're planning on using the crate to housetrain your dog — because he will eliminate in one corner and lie down in another. Get a crate that is big enough for your dog when he is an adult.

Then, use dividers to limit the space for when he's a puppy.

◆ **Bed:** A plush doggie bed will make sleeping and resting more comfortable for your toy dog. Dog beds come in all shapes, sizes and colors, but your dog just needs one that is soft and large enough for him to stretch out on. Because puppies and rescue dogs often don't come housetrained, it's helpful to buy a bed that can be washed easily. If your toy dog will be sleeping in a crate, a nice crate pad and a small blanket that he can burrow in will help him feel more at home. Replace the blanket if it becomes ragged and starts to fall apart because your toy dog's nails could get caught in it.

◆ **Gate:** Similar to those used for toddlers, gates help keep your toy dog confined to one room or area when you can't supervise him. Gates also work to keep your Chihuahua out

Are you prepared for your Chi to become part of your household?

Think like a little dog when preparing the house for your new arrival. Block off places that could get your Chi in trouble.

of areas you don't want him in. Gates are available in many sizes and styles. For toy dogs, make sure the one you choose has openings small enough so your puppy can't squeeze through the bars or any openings.

◆ **Toys:** Keep your dog occupied and entertained by providing him with an array of fun and engaging toys. Teething

SMART TIP!

When you are unable to watch your toy puppy, put her in a crate or an exercise pen on an easily cleanable floor. If she does have an accident on carpeting, clean it completely and meticulously, so that it won't smell like his potty.

puppies like to chew — in fact, chewing is a physical need for pups as they are teething — and everything from your shoes to the leather couch to the fancy rug is fair game. Divert your Chi's chewing instincts with durable toys like bones made of nylon or hard rubber.

Other fun toys include rope toys, treat-dispensing toys and balls. Make sure the toys and bones don't have small parts that could break off and be swallowed, causing your dog to choke. Stuffed toys can become destuffed and an overly excited toy puppy may ingest the stuffing or the squeaker. Check your Chihuahua's toys regularly and replace them if they become frayed or show signs of wear.

◆ **Cleaning supplies:** Until your Chihuahua pup is housetrained, you will be

NOTABLE & QUOTABLE

Playing with toys from puppyhood encourages good behavior and social skills throughout your dog's life. A happy, playful dog is a content and well-adjusted one. Also, because all puppies chew to soothe their gums and help loosen puppy teeth, dogs should always have easy access to several different toys.

— dog trainer and author Harrison Forbes, Savannah, Tenn.

doing a lot of cleaning. Potty accidents will occur, which is acceptable in the beginning because your Chihuahua puppy won't know any better. All you can do is be prepared to clean up any accidents with a positive attitude. Old rags, towels, newspapers and a stain-and-odor remover are good to have on hand.

BEYOND THE BASICS

The items mentioned are the bare necessities. You will find out what else you need as you go along — grooming supplies, flea/tick protection, etc. These things will vary depending on your situation, but it is important that you have everything you need to make your Chi comfortable in his new home.

With careful planning and preparation, you'll have your Chihuahua feeling at home in no time!

HOUSETRAINING

Unexciting as it may be, the house-training part of puppy rearing greatly affects the budding relationship between a smart owner and his puppy — particularly when it becomes an area of ongoing contention. Fortunately, armed with suitable knowledge, patience and common sense, you'll find housetraining progresses at a relatively smooth rate. That leaves more time for the important things, like cuddling your adorable puppy, showing him off and laughing at his numerous antics.

Successful housetraining begins with total supervision and management until you know your dog has developed a preference for outside surfaces — grass, gravel, concrete — instead of carpet, tile or hardwood. Crates, tethers, exercise pens and leashes are tools that will help accomplish this. Be consistent, and your puppy will soon know that potty-ing should occur outside.

IN THE BEGINNING

For the first two to three weeks of a puppy's life, his mother helps him to eliminate. His mother also keeps the whelping

it's a **Fact**

Ongoing housetraining difficulties may indicate that your puppy has a health problem, warranting an immediate veterinary checkup. A urinary infection, parasites, a virus and other nasty issues greatly affect your puppy's ability to hold it.

box, or "nest area," clean. When pups begin to walk around and eat on their own, they choose where they eliminate. You can train your puppy to relieve himself wherever you choose, but this must be somewhere suitable. You should keep in mind from the start that when your Chi puppy is old enough to go out in public places, any canine deposits must be removed at once; always carry a small plastic bag or poop scoop.

When deciding on the surface and location that you will want your Chihuahua to use, be sure it is going to be permanent. Training your dog on grass and then changing two months later is extremely difficult for your dog to comprehend.

Next, choose the cue you will use each and every time you want your puppy to potty. "Let's go," "hurry up" and "potty" are examples of cues commonly used by smart dog owners. Get in the habit of giving your puppy the chosen relief cue before you take him out. That way, when he becomes an adult, you will be able to determine if he wants to go out when you ask him. A confirmation will be signs of interest, such as wagging his tail, watching you intently or going to the door.

LET'S START WITH THE CRATE

Clean animals by nature, dogs keenly dislike soiling where they sleep and eat. This fact makes a crate a useful tool for housetraining. When purchasing a crate, consider that one correctly sized will allow adequate room for an adult dog to stand full-height, lie on his side without scrunching and turn around easily. If debating plastic versus wire crates, short-haired breeds sometimes prefer the warmer, draft-blocking quality of plastic while furry dogs often like the cooling airflow of a wire crate.

Some crates come equipped with a movable wall that reduces the interior size to provide enough space for your puppy to stand, turn and lie down, but that do not allow room to soil one end and sleep in the other. The problem is, if your puppy potties in the crate anyway, the divider forces him to lie in his own excrement. This can work against you by desensitizing your puppy against his normal, instinctive revulsion to resting where he has eliminated. If scheduling permits you or a responsible family member to clean the crate soon after it's soiled, then you can continue cratetraining because limiting crate size does encourage your Chi puppy to hold it. Otherwise, give him enough room to move away from an unclean area until he's better able to control his urge to potty.

Needless to say, not every puppy adheres to this guideline. If your Chi moves along at a faster pace, thank your lucky stars. Should he progress slower, accept it and remind yourself that he'll improve. Be aware that pups frequently hold it longer at night than during the day. Just because your puppy sleeps for six or more hours through the night, it does not mean he can hold it that long during the more active daytime hours.

One last bit of advice on the crate: Place it in the corner of a normally trafficked room, such as the family room or kitchen. Social and curious by nature, dogs like to feel

Did You Know? Clean accidents thoroughly with an enzyme solution to dramatically reduce the time it takes to house-train your dog because she won't be drawn back to the same areas.

Reward your Chi while inside his crate to help him associate the crate with positive experiences.

included in family happenings. Creating a quiet retreat by putting the crate in an unused area may seem like a good idea, but results in your puppy feeling insecure and isolated. Watching his people pop in and out of his crate room reassures your puppy that he's not forgotten.

Remember, one of the primary ingredients in housetraining your puppy is control. Regardless of your lifestyle, there will always be occasions when you will need to have a place where your dog can stay and be happy and safe. Cratetraining is the answer for now and in the future.

PUPPY'S NEEDS

Your puppy needs to relieve himself after play periods, after each meal, after he has been sleeping and any time he indicates that he is looking for a place to urinate or defecate. If you notice your Chi sniffing around and getting antsy, that's your cue to take him to his potty place so he can eliminate.

The urinary and intestinal tract muscles of very young puppies are not fully developed. Therefore, like human babies, puppies need to relieve themselves frequently. Take your puppy out often — every hour for an 8-week-old, for example — and always immediately after sleeping and eating. The older the puppy, the less often he will need to relieve himself. As a mature, healthy adult, he will require only three to five relief trips per day.

HOUSING HELP

Because the types of housing and control you provide for your Chihuahua puppy have a direct relationship on housetraining success, you must consider the various aspects of both before beginning training. Taking a new puppy home and turning him loose in your house can be compared to turning a child loose in a sports arena and telling the child that the place is all his! The sheer enormity of the place would be too much for him to handle. Instead, offer your puppy clearly defined areas where he can play, sleep, eat and live. A room of the house where the family gathers is the most obvious choice.

NOTABLE & QUOTABLE *Reward your pup with a high-value treat immediately after she potties to reinforce going in the proper location, then play for a short time afterward. This teaches that good things happen after pottying outside!* — Victoria Schade a certified pet dog trainer from Annandale, Va.

Did You Know?

White vinegar is a good odor remover if you don't have any professional cleaners on hand. Use one-quarter cup mixed with one quart of water.

Puppies are social animals, and they need to feel like they are a part of the pack right from the start. Hearing your voice and watching you go about your business positively reinforces your pup's status as a member of your pack. A family room, kitchen or a nearby adjoining area is ideal for providing safety and security for Chi puppy and owner.

Within that room, there should be a smaller area that your Chihuahua puppy can call his own. An alcove, a wire or fiberglass dog crate or a fenced (not boarded!) corner from which he can view the activities of his new family will be fine. The size of the area or crate is the key factor here. The area must be large enough for the puppy to lie down and stretch out his body, yet small enough so he cannot relieve himself at one end and sleep at the other without coming into contact with his droppings before he is fully trained to relieve himself outside.

Dogs are, by nature, clean animals and will not remain close to their relief areas unless forced to do so. In those cases, they

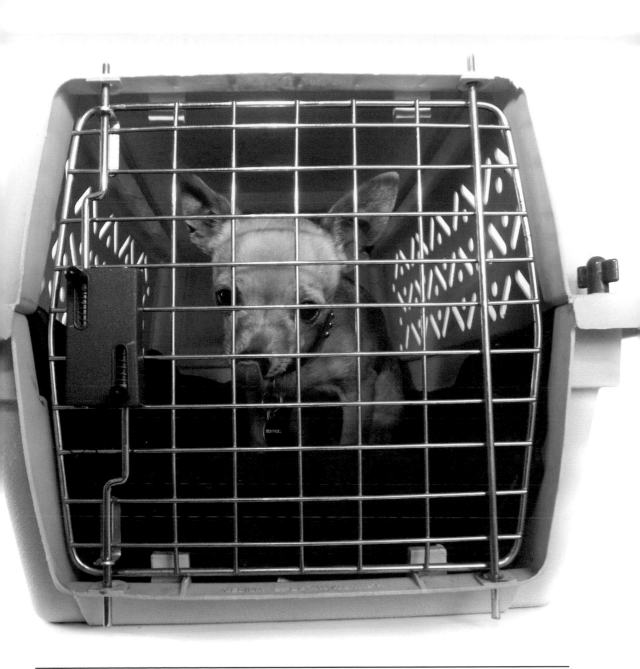

How often does a Chihuahua puppy do his business? A lot! Go to **DogChannel.com/Club-Chi** and download the typical potty schedule of a puppy. You can also download a chart that you can fill out to track your dog's elimination timetable, which will help you with housetraining.

JOIN OUR
ONLINE
**Club
Chi™**

SMART TIP!

If you acquire your puppy at 8 weeks of age, expect to take her out at least six to eight times a day. By the time she's about 6 months old, potty trips will be down to three or four times a day. A rule of thumb is to take your Chihuahua puppy out in hourly intervals equal to her age in months.

then go against their natural instinct to avoid their droppings and become dirty dogs and usually remain that way for life.

His designated area should be lined with clean bedding and a toy. Water must always be available, in a no-spill container, once your dog is reliably housetrained.

IN CONTROL

By control, we mean helping your toy puppy to create a lifestyle pattern that will be compatible with that of his pack (that's you!). Just as we guide children to learn our way of life, we must show our pup when it is time to play, eat, sleep, exercise and entertain himself.

Your puppy should always sleep in his crate. He should also learn that, during times

Top Tips

10 HOUSETRAINING HOW-TOs

1. Decide where you want your dog to eliminate and take her there every time until she gets the idea. Pick a spot that's easy to access. Remember, puppies have very little time between "gotta go" and "oops."

2. Teach an elimination cue, such as "go potty" or "get busy." Say this every time you take your Chi to eliminate. Don't keep chanting the cue. Just say it once or twice; then, keep quiet so you won't distract your dog.

3. Praise calmly when your dog eliminates, but stand there a little longer in case there's more.

4. Keep potty outings for potty only. Take your dog to the designated spot, tell her "go potty" and just stand there. If she needs to eliminate, she will do so within five minutes.

5. Don't punish for potty accidents; punishment can hinder progress. If you catch your toy dog in the act indoors, verbally interrupt but don't scold. Gently lead your pup to the approved spot, let her finish, then praise.

6. If it's too late to interrupt an accident, scoop the poop or blot up the urine with a paper towel. Immediately take your Chihuahua and her deposit (gently!) to the potty area.

Place the poop or trace of urine on the ground and praise the pup. If she sniffs at her waste, praise more. Let your dog know you're pleased when her waste is in the proper area.

7. Keep track of when and where your Chi eliminates. That will help you anticipate potty times. Regular meals mean regular elimination, so feed your dog scheduled, measured meals instead of free-feeding (leaving food available at all times).

8. Hang a bell on a sturdy cord from the doorknob. Before you open the door to take your dog out for potty, shake the string and ring the bell. Most dogs will soon realize the connection between the bell ringing and the door opening, then they'll try it out for themselves. Listen for that bell!

9. Dogs naturally return to where they've previously eliminated, so thoroughly clean up all indoor accidents. Household cleaners usually will do the job, but special enzyme solutions may work better.

10. If the ground is littered with too much waste, your toy dog may seek a cleaner place to eliminate. Scoop the potty area daily, leaving just one "reminder."

of household confusion and excessive human activity, such as at breakfast when family members are preparing for the day, he can play by himself in relative safety and in the comfort of his designated area. Each time you leave your Chihuahua alone, he should understand exactly where he is to stay.

Other times of excitement, such as parties, can be fun for your Chihuahua, provided that he can view the activities from the security of his designated area. This way, your dog will not be underfoot and he will not be fed all sorts of table scraps that probably will cause stomach distress, yet he will still feel like he's a part of the fun.

SCHEDULE A SOLUTION

Your puppy should be taken to his relief area each time he is released from his designated area, after meals, after play sessions and when he first awakens in the morning (at 8 weeks, this can mean 5 a.m.!). Your Chi puppy will indicate that he's ready "to go" by circling or sniffing busily; do not misinterpret these signs. For a puppy younger than 10 weeks of age, a routine of taking him out every hour is necessary. As the puppy grows older, he will be able to wait for longer periods of time without having to eliminate.

Keep trips to your puppy's relief area short. Stay no more than five or six minutes; then, return to the house. If he goes during that time, praise him lavishly and immediately take him indoors. If he does not, but he has an accident when you go back indoors, pick

him up immediately, say "No!" and return to his relief area. Wait a few minutes, then return to the house again. Never spank your puppy or rub his face in urine or excrement when he has had an accident. In fact, you should never hit your puppy as a form of punishment. This will cause him to fear you and harm your relationship.

Once indoors, put your puppy in his crate until you have had time to clean up his accident. Then release him to the family area and watch him more closely than before. Chances are, his accident was a result of your not picking up his potty signals or waiting too long before offering him the opportunity to relieve himself. Never hold a grudge against your puppy for accidents.

Let the puppy learn that going outdoors means it is time to relieve himself, not to play. Once trained, he will be able to play indoors and out and differentiate between the times for play versus the times for relief.

Smart owners will help their Chihuahua puppies develop regular hours for naps, being alone, playing by himself and simply resting — all in his crate. Encourage your puppy to entertain himself while you are busy. Let him learn that having you nearby is comforting, but it is not your main purpose in life to provide him with undivided attention.

Each time you put your Chi puppy in his area, use the same cue that suits you best. Soon, he will run to his crate or special area when he hears you say those special words.

A few key elements are really all you need for a successful housetraining method — consistency, frequency, praise, control and supervision. By following these procedures with a normal, healthy puppy, you and your Chihuahua will soon be past the stage of accidents and ready to move on to a full, rewarding life together.

it's a **Fact**

Dogs are descendants of wolves. So you can think of your Chihuahua's crate as a modern-day den.

JOIN OUR ONLINE Club Chi™

Having housetraining problems with your toy dog? Ask other Chihuahua owners for advice and tips. Log onto **DogChannel.com/ Club-Chi** and click on "Community."

CHAPTER 6

VET VISITS AND

EVERYDAY CARE

Your selection of a veterinarian should be based on personal recommendation considering the doctor's skills with dogs, specifically Chihuahuas if possible. Following are important things to keep in mind while you search for a veterinarian whom you can trust to care for your precious Chihuahua.

FIRST STEP: SELECT THE RIGHT VET

All licensed veterinarians are trained to deal with routine medical issues, such as infections and injuries, and administer vaccinations. If the problem affecting your Chi is more complex, your vet will refer you to someone with more detailed knowledge of what is wrong. This usually will be a specialist like a veterinary dermatologist, veterinary ophthalmologist or whichever specialty service you require.

Veterinary procedures can be very costly and, as the available treatments improve, they are only going to become more expensive. It is quite acceptable to discuss matters of cost with your veterinarian; if there is more than one treatment option available, cost may be a factor in deciding which treatment route to take.

Smart owners will search for a veterinarian before they actually need one. New pet owners should start looking a month or two before they bring home their new Chihuahua. This will give them time to meet candidate veterinarians, check out the condition of the clinic, meet the staff and decide who they feel most comfortable with. If you already have a Chi puppy, look sooner rather than later, preferably not in the midst of a veterinary health crisis.

Second, define the criteria that are important to you. Points to consider or investigate:

Convenience: Proximity to your home, extended hours or drop-off services are helpful for owners who work regular business hours, have a busy schedule or do not want to drive far. If you have mobility issues, finding a vet who makes house calls or a service that provides pet transport might be particularly important.

Size: A one-person practice ensures you will always deal with the same vet during each visit. "That person can really get to know both you and your dog," says Bernadine Cruz, D.V.M., of Laguna Hills Animal Hospital in Laguna Hills, Calif. The downside, though, is that the sole practitioner does not have the immediate input of another vet, and if your vet becomes ill or takes time off, you may be out of luck.

The multiple-doctor practice offers consistency if your Chihuahua needs to come in unexpectedly on a day when your veterinarian isn't there. Additionally, your vet can quickly consult with his colleagues at the clinic if he's unsure about a diagnosis or a type of treatment.

If you find a veterinarian within that practice whom you really like, you can make your appointments with that individual, establishing the same kind of bond that you would with a solo practitioner.

Appointment Policies: Some veterinarian practices are strictly by-appointment only, which could minimize your wait time. However, if a sudden problem arises with your Chi and the veterinarians are booked, they might not be able to squeeze your dog in that day. Some clinics are walk-in only, great for crisis or impromptu visits, but without scheduling may involve longer waits to see the next available veterinarian — whoever is open, not someone in particular. Some practices offer the best of both worlds by maintaining an appointment schedule but also keep slots open throughout the day for walk-ins.

Basic vs. State-of-the-Art vs. Full Service: A practice with high-tech equipment offers greater diagnostic capabilities and treatment options, important for tricky or difficult cases. However, the cost of pricey equipment is passed along to the client, so you could pay more for routine procedures —

the bulk of most pets' appointments. Some practices offer boarding, grooming, training classes and other services on the premises — conveniences many pet owners appreciate.

Fees and Payment Polices: How much does a routine office call cost? If there is a significant price difference, ask why. If you intend to carry health insurance on your Chihuahua or want to pay by credit card, make sure the candidate clinic accepts those payment options.

FIRST VET VISIT

It is much easier, less costly and more effective to practice preventive health care than to fight bouts of illness and disease. Properly bred puppies of all breeds come from parents who were selected based upon their genetic disease profile. The puppies' mother should have been vaccinated, free

of all internal and external parasites and properly nourished. For these reasons, a visit to the veterinarian who cared for the dam (mother) is recommended if possible. The dam passes her disease resistance to her

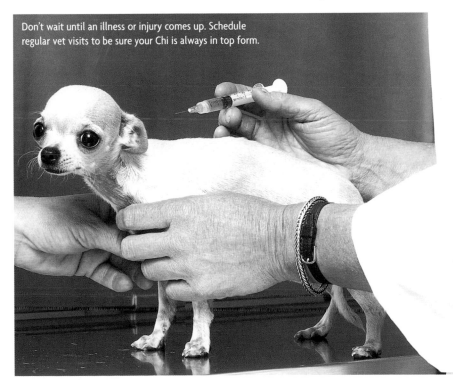

Don't wait until an illness or injury comes up. Schedule regular vet visits to be sure your Chi is always in top form.

puppies, which should last from eight to 10 weeks. Unfortunately, she can also pass on parasites and infection. This is why knowledge about her health is useful in learning more about the health of her puppies.

Now that you have your Chihuahua puppy home safe and sound, it's time to arrange your pup's first trip to the veterinarian. Perhaps the breeder can recommend someone in the area who specializes in Chis, or maybe you know other Chihuahua owners who can suggest a good vet. Either way, you should make an appointment within a couple of days of bringing home your puppy. If possible, stop by for this first vet appointment before going home.

The pup's first vet visit will consist of an overall examination to make sure that he does not have any problems that are not apparent to you. The veterinarian also will set up a schedule for your pup's vaccinations; the breeder will inform you of which ones your dog has already received and the vet can continue from there.

Your Chi will also have his teeth examined and have his skeletal conformation and general health checked prior to certification by the veterinarian. Puppies in certain breeds have problems with their kneecaps, cataracts and other eye problems, heart murmurs and undescended testicles. They may also have personality problems; your veterinarian might even have training in temperament evaluation.

VACCINATION SCHEDULING

Most vaccinations are given by injection and should only be given by a veterinarian. Both you and the vet should keep a record of the date of the injection, the identification of the vaccine and the amount given. Some vets give a first vaccination at 8 weeks of age, but most dog breeders prefer the course

not to commence until about 10 weeks because of interaction with the antibodies produced by the mother. The vaccination scheduling is usually based on a 15-day cycle. You must take your vet's advice as to when to vaccinate, as this may differ according to the vaccine used.

The usual vaccines contain immunizing doses of several different viruses such as distemper, parvovirus, parainfluenza and hepatitis. There are other vaccines available when the puppy is at risk; you should rely on your vet's advice. This is especially true for

Set up a vet visit before you bring your new dog home, so you can meet and interview the veterinarian staff.

NOTABLE & QUOTABLE

Some toy breeds have bad knees, and others can break a leg jumping off furniture. Those little bones don't always mend well. My rule is that if they can't get up on something themselves, they shouldn't be up there.

— Julie Clemen, owner of Little Paws Boarding in Olympia, Wash.

the booster immunizations. Most vaccination programs require a booster when the puppy is a year old and once a year thereafter. In some cases, circumstances may require more frequent immunizations.

Kennel cough, more formally known as *tracheobronchitis*, is immunized with a vaccine that is sprayed into the dog's nostrils. Kennel cough is usually included in routine vaccinations, but it's usually not as effective as vaccines for other diseases.

Your veterinarian probably will recommend that your Chihuahua puppy be fully vaccinated before you take him on outings. There are airborne diseases, parasite eggs in the grass and unexpected visits from other dogs that might be dangerous to your puppy's health. Other dogs are the most harmful reservoir of pathogenic organisms, as everything they have can be transmitted to your puppy.

6 Months to 1 Year of Age: Unless you intend to breed or show your dog, neutering/spaying your puppy at 6 months of age is recommended. Discuss this with your veterinarian. Neutering/spaying has proven to be beneficial to male and female puppies, respectively. Besides eliminating the possibility of pregnancy, it inhibits (but does not prevent) breast cancer in females and prostate cancer in male dogs.

Your veterinarian should provide your Chihuahua puppy with a thorough dental evaluation

at 6 months, ascertaining whether all his permanent teeth have come in properly. A home dental care regimen should be initiated at 6 months, including brushing weekly and providing good dental devices (such as nylon bones). Regular dental care promotes healthy teeth, fresh breath and a longer life.

Dogs Older Than 1 Year: Visit the veterinarian at least once a year. There is no such disease as "old age," but bodily functions do change as your dog gets older. Their eyes and ears are no longer as efficient, and liver, kidney and intestinal functions begin to decline. Proper dietary changes recommended by your veterinarian can make life pleasant for your aging Chi and you.

NOTABLE & QUOTABLE

Be careful about babying toy breeds too much because these dogs can become spoiled in a heartbeat. If you don't train out the aggressive, protective tendency, you can get an armpit piranha [a dog who snaps and bites at people, especially while being held in the crook of his owner's arm]. As small as they are, you can be liable if they bite someone, and it's not pleasant to get bitten by a Chihuahua.

— Bruce Shirky, a Chihuahua breeder in San Antonio, Texas

When selecting a veterinarian, make sure he or she is familiar with Chihuahuas.

Chis are muy bueno!

We Love Toy Dogs

EVERYDAY HAPPENINGS

Keeping your Chihuahua healthy is a matter of keen observation and quick action when necessary. Knowing what's normal for your dog will help you recognize signs of trouble before they blossom into a full-blown emergency situation.

Even if it is a minor problem, such as a cut or scrape, you'll want to care for it immediately to prevent infection, and to ensure your dog doesn't make it worse by chewing or scratching at it. Here's what to do for minor injuries or illnesses and how to recognize and deal with emergencies.

Cuts and Scrapes: For a cut or scrape that's half an inch or smaller, clean the wound with saline solution or warm water and use tweezers to remove any splinters or other debris. Apply antibiotic ointment. No bandage is necessary unless the wound is on a paw, which can pick up dirt when your dog walks on it. Deep cuts with lots of bleeding or those caused by glass or some other object should be treated by your veterinarian.

Cold Symptoms: Dogs don't actually get colds, but they can get illnesses that have similar symptoms, such as coughing, a runny nose or sneezing. Dogs cough for any num-

Just like with infants, puppies need a series of vaccinations during their first year of life to ensure that they stay healthy. Download a vaccination chart from **DogChannel.com/Club-Chi** that you can fill out for your Chihuahua.

ber of reasons, from respiratory infections to inhaled irritants to congestive heart failure. Take your Chi to the veterinarian for prolonged coughing or coughing accompanied by labored breathing, runny eyes or nose or bloody phlegm.

A runny nose that continues for more than several hours requires veterinary attention, as well. If your Chihuahua sneezes, he may have some mild nasal irritation that will go away on its own, but frequent sneezing, especially if it's accompanied by a runny nose, may indicate anything from allergies to an infection to something stuck in the nose.

Vomiting and Diarrhea: Sometimes dogs suffer minor gastric upset when they eat a new type of food, eat too much, eat the contents of the trash can or become excited or anxious. Give your Chi's stomach a rest by withholding food for 12 hours, and then feeding him a bland diet such as baby food, or rice and chicken, gradually returning your Chihuahua to his normal food.

Projectile vomiting, or vomiting and diarrhea that continues for more than 48 hours, is another matter. If this happens, take your Chi to the veterinarian immediately.

MORE HEALTH HINTS

A Chihuahua's anal glands can cause problems if not periodically evacuated. In the wild, dogs regularly clear their anal glands to mark their territory, but in domestic dogs this function is no longer necessary; thus, their contents can build up and clog, causing discomfort. Signs that the anal glands — located on both sides of the anus — need emptying

are if a Chi drags his rear end along the ground or keeps turning around to attend to the uncomfortable patch.

While care must be taken not to cause injury, anal glands can be evacuated by gently pressing on either side of the anal opening and by using a piece of cotton or a tissue to collect the foul-smelling matter. If anal glands are allowed to become impacted, abscesses can form, causing pain and the need for veterinary attention.

Chihuahuas can get into all sorts of mischief, so it's not uncommon for them to inadvertently swallow something poisonous in the course of their investigations. Obviously, an urgent visit to your vet is required under such circumstances, but if possible, when you telephone him or her, you should advise which poisonous substance has been ingested, as different treatments are needed. Should it be necessary to cause your dog to vomit (which is not always the case with poisoning), a small lump of baking soda, given orally, will have an immediate effect. Alternatively, a teaspoon of salt or mustard, dissolved in water, will have a similar effect but may be more difficult to administer and not as quick to take effect.

Chihuahua puppies often have painful fits while they are teething. These are not usually serious and are brief, caused only by the pain of teething. Of course, you must be certain that the cause is not more serious, so keep a close eye on the incoming teeth. Giving a puppy something hard to chew on will usually be enough to solve this temporary teething problem.

JOIN OUR ONLINE Club Chi™

No matter how careful you are with your precious Chihuahua, sometimes unexpected injuries happen. Be prepared for any emergency by assembling a canine first-aid kit. Find out what essentials you need on **DogChannel.com/Club-Chi** — just click on "Downloads."

A healthy Chihuahua starts with a responsible owner. Stay on top of your Chi's vet visits and keep a record of all his vaccinations.

CHAPTER 7

ON THE TOPIC

The best way to ensure good health for your Chihuahua is by maintaining a consistent wellness program. Take your dog in for regular veterinary exams, stay current with his vaccinations and flea or heartworm prevention (per your veterinarian's recommendation), keep your Chi's skin and coat groomed and clean, brush your dog's teeth regularly and seek prompt veterinary attention if your dog exhibits physical or behavioral changes.

The latter is a key component to your Chihuahua's health. Staying on top of developing problems via early diagnosis and treatment often yields the best prognosis, by either correcting a problem before it becomes severe or permanent, or for life-ending diseases, by helping slow disease progression and extending your dog's remaining months or years.

Although the Chihuahua is a healthy breed with a lifespan of anywhere from 12 to 18 years, the breed is not immune to genetic problems — no mixed or purebred dog is. In fact, all domestic and wild mammals, including humans, carry some defective genes that may or may not manifest into a full-blown disease. Some of the disorders seen in the Chi include luxated patellas, tracheal collapse, congestive heart disease and hypogyclemia.

Did You Know? **Dogs can get many diseases from ticks,** including Lyme disease, Rocky Mountain spotted fever, tick bite paralysis and others.

BAD KNEES

Patellar luxation (slipped kneecap), an orthopedic problem seen in many smaller breeds, is one of the most common causes of lameness. It's usually caused by abnormalities in the patella (a flat, movable bone at the front of the knee) and is a hereditary disorder. Generally, the problem starts when the dog is still young, 6 months or younger, although occasionally an older dog will be affected. Trauma to the knee can also force the patella out of place — something that can happen at any age.

When the patella luxates, the rear lower leg seems to momentarily lock and the dog "skips" for a stride or two; then the leg drops back into place again and everything is fine. Often, the skipping gait occurs while the dog is trotting or directly after he first stands, turns or jumps.

Depending upon how advanced the problem becomes, a dog can experience discomfort, lameness and permanent joint damage, so it's best not to ignore this condition. A veterinary exam is important to confirm the diagnosis (which is based on a physical exam and radiographs) and to evaluate the severity of the problem as soon as possible.

In mild cases where the patella only very occasionally dislocates and pops right back in the groove, there is no residual lameness, very little discomfort and little or no cumulative or permanent damage to the joint, making treatment unnecessary. You should monitor your pet, however, and have him re-evaluated if the luxations become more frequent or the patella stays out of the groove for longer periods of time.

In some cases, the patella luxates more frequently, doesn't slip back into the groove quickly or the veterinarian determines that the patella pops out too easily. These dogs need surgery to correct the condition and to prevent permanent lameness and joint damage.

In these cases, without treatment, a dog will not get better on his own, and the condition could worsen, causing more pain and greater damage to the joint. The more damage a joint undergoes, the more difficult it is to repair the abnormalities and to achieve complete surgical correction.

To prevent over-exercising, keep your dog on a leash when taken outside to relieve himself and crated at other times. As your dog recovers, leash walks and gradually increased exercise are permitted, per veterinary evaluation. Usually, dogs complete their recovery in a couple of months. When treated promptly, prognosis for a full recovery is usually good.

COUGHING AND FATIGUE

Your Chihuahua is coughing, is unusually fatigued after play or exercise, and has trouble breathing. Your veterinarian listens to your dog's heart, detects abnormal heart sounds and after additional diagnostics, says your little dog has congestive heart failure, a condition in which the heart becomes weak and inefficient. What does this mean for your pet?

SMART TIP!

Many skin irritations can be prevented or reduced by employing a simple preventive regimen:
- Keep your Chi clean and dry.
- Bathe her regularly (especially during allergy season) with a hypoallergenic shampoo.
- Rinse her coat thoroughly.
- Practice good flea control.
- Supplement her diet with fatty acids.

CHF is a broad, umbrella term used to describe specific cardiac diseases. The major cardiac problem seen in older Chihuahuas is left-sided valvular disease, also called mitral valve disease. This is a disorder in which the heart valve slowly thickens and becomes deformed, causing the valve to leak; a soft murmur is often heard with this leakage. Chihuahuas have a genetic predisposition for this disease.

Other causes of CHF are poor dental health (bacteria in the mouth can travel through the bloodstream and cause abnormalities on the heart valves) and heartworm disease.

After hearing abnormal heart sounds, your veterinarian may perform blood work, a urinalysis and take chest X-rays. The vet may also perform an echocardiogram (a cardiac ultrasound to evaluate heart pumping) or an electrocardiogram (an EKG, which measures the rate and regularity of heartbeats). These tests will evaluate the overall health of your pet, and the diseases of the heart, allowing your veterinarian to prescribe appropriate treatment.

Your veterinarian will recommend various drugs and management tools to help control your dog's condition. Depending on your dog's needs, these might include some of the following:

- Diuretics can remove some of the excess fluid in the body that cause swelling.
- Vasodilators widen blood vessels and lower blood pressure, making it easier for the heart to pump blood.
- Digoxin improves the ability of the heart to pump blood.
- Reduced-salt diets minimize the need for diuretics and reduce fluid retention in the lungs. Special diets are available or your veterinarian can help you plan home-cooked meals.
- Restricted exercise helps prevent over-exertion of the heart.

CHF cannot be cured and the prognosis is guarded. If detected early, your pet can be made comfortable and survive for many years. If the disease is diagnosed in later stages, life expectancy for your dog could be as little as a few months.

BREATHING DIFFICULTIES

Sometimes your dog may exhibit a dry, honking cough after excitement or play. After exercise or a big burst of excitement, your Chi might have labored breathing, be overly fatigued, even faint. The honking cough and these other clinical signs suggest your dog could have a tracheal collapse. This condition is a malformation seen in small dogs in which structures inside the trachea (also known as the windpipe) aren't stiff enough to hold the trachea open as the dog breaths. When your dog starts rapidly inhaling air, such as during physical activity or excitement, the trachea flattens, obstructs the airway and restricts oxygen to the lungs.

"We're not completely sure why this condition occurs," says Lila Miller, D.V.M., veterinary advisor and senior director for animal sciences for the American Society for the Prevention of Cruelty to Animals. Dogs are often born with the condition, but it's believed that other airway disorders could lead to tracheal collapse. Additionally, poor-quality dog food could be a contributor

because proper nutrients are needed for the proper formation of airway structures. Some contributing factors include allergies, obesity, cigarette smoke and other environmental irritants.

A diagnosis is made through tracheal X-rays, endoscopy, history, clinical signs and a physical examination.

Depending on how affected your dog is, your veterinarian will recommend drug therapy to control clinical signs, lifestyle changes to minimize physical stress on the respiratory system or surgery to implant a device that keeps the airway open, Miller says.

Although drug therapy doesn't correct the disorder, it can be successful in managing the disease in many dogs. "We use a lot of different drug therapies," Miller says. "Cough suppressants to reduce irritation, tranquilizers to keep a high-strung dog from getting overly excited, bronchodilators to help the animal breathe better or perhaps steroids to reduce inflammation. If there's a secondary infection going on, we'll prescribe antibiotics."

If necessary, your veterinarian may also recommend making a few changes to your dog's activities. You might need to limit your Chihuahua's exercise and play, avoid exercises that involve running or jumping. When walking your dog, walk him in a harness instead of a collar, which puts pressure on the trachea when your dog pulls. You'll also need to help your Chi shed the extra pounds if he's overweight. "Being overweight stresses the cardiovascular and respiratory systems," Miller warns.

Most dogs respond well to drug and management therapy. "In most cases, the dog is not in distress all the time: Usually the condition is exacerbated by exercise and excitement," Miller says. "If he's running around and barking, he may have an episode with a lot of coughing, then it subsides. It's really only in severe cases where dogs have distress that is exacerbated by normal activity."

In severe cases in which the dog faints or turns blue from lack of oxygen, and the disease doesn't respond well to medical management and lifestyle changes, your veterinarian may suggest surgery to implant a prosthetic device that holds the trachea open in a normal position. Miller notes that only an expert should perform tracheal surgery and the surgery is not without risk. "But if the surgery is successful, the dog can lead a normal life," she says.

AUTO-IMMUNE ILLNESS

An auto-immune illness is one in which the immune system overacts and does not recognize parts of the affected dog. Instead, the immune system starts to react and turns against the body's cells as if they were foreign cells and therefore must be destroyed. An example is rheumatoid arthritis, which occurs when the body does not recognize the joints, which leads to a very painful and damaging reaction in the joints. This has nothing to do with age, so it can occur in puppies. The wear-and-tear arthritis in elderly people or dogs is called osteoarthritis.

Lupus is another auto-immune disease that affects dogs as well as people. It can take various forms, affecting the kidneys, bones and skin. It can be fatal, but is treated with steroids, which can unfortunately trigger very harsh side effects. Steroids calm down the allergic reaction to the body's tissues, which helps the lupus, but it also calms down the body's reaction to actual foreign substances such as bacteria — making your dog vulnerable to other illnesses. Steroids also weakens the skin and bones.

Did You Know? Across the globe, more than 800 species of ticks exist, and they aren't particular to where they dine. Mammals, birds and reptiles are all fair game.

FOOD ALLERGIES

Feeding your Chihuahua properly is very important. An improper diet could affect your dog's health, behavior and nervous system, possibly making a normal dog aggressive. The result of a good or bad diet is most visible in a dog's skin and coat, but internal organs are affected, too.

Dogs can be allergic to many foods that are popular and even recommended by breeders and veterinarians. Changing the brand of food may not eliminate the problem if the ingredient to which your dog is allergic to is in the new brand.

Recognizing a food allergy can be difficult. Humans often have rashes or swelling of the lips or eyes when they eat foods they are allergic to. Dogs do not usually develop rashes, but they react the same way they do to an airborne allergy or insect bite; they itch, scratch and bite. While pollen allergies and parasite bites are usually seasonal, food allergies are continual problems.

Diagnosis of a food allergy is based on a 2- to 4-week dietary trial with a diet of home-cooked food, excluding all other foods. The diet should consist of boiled rice or potato with a protein source your Chihuahua has never eaten before, such as fresh or frozen fish, lamb or even something as exotic as pheasant. Water has to be the only drink, and it is important that no other foods are fed during this trial. If your dog's condition improves, try the original diet again to see if the itching resumes. If it does, then your dog is allergic to his original diet. You must find a diet that does not distress your Chi's

Just like some humans, some Chis suffer from food allergies.

skin. Start with a commercially available hypoallergenic diet or the homemade diet that you created for the allergy trial.

Food intolerance is your dog's inability to completely digest certain foods. This occurs because the dog does not have the enzymes necessary to digest some foodstuffs. All puppies have the enzymes necessary to digest canine milk, but some dogs do not have the enzymes to digest cow milk, resulting in loose bowels, stomach pains and flatulence.

Dogs often do not have the enzymes to digest soy or other beans. These foods should be excluded from your Chihuahua's diet.

PARASITE BITES

Insect bites itch, erupt and may even become infected. Dogs have the same reaction to fleas, ticks and mites. When an insect lands on you, you can whisk it away with your hand. Unfortunately, when a dog is bitten by a flea, tick or mite he can only scratch or bite.

By the time your Chihuahua has been bitten, the parasite has done its damage. It may also have laid eggs, which will cause further problems. The itching from parasite bites is probably due to the saliva injected into the site when the parasite sucks the dog's blood.

EXTERNAL PARASITES

Fleas: Of all the problems to which dogs are prone, none is better known and more frustrating than fleas. Flea infestation is relatively simple to cure but difficult to prevent.

To control flea infestation, you have to understand the flea's life cycle. Fleas are often thought of as a summertime problem, but centrally heated homes have made fleas a year-round problem. The most effective method of treating fleas is a two-stage approach: Kill the adult fleas, then control the development of

Brush your dog's teeth every day. Plaque colonizes on the tooth surface in as little as six to eight hours, and if not removed by brushing, forms calculus (tartar) within three to five days. Plaque and tartar cause gum disease, periodontal disease, loosening of the teeth and tooth loss. In bad cases of dental disease, bacteria from the mouth can get into the bloodstream, leading to kidney or heart problems — both of which are life-shortening.

pre-adult fleas (*pupae*). Unfortunately, no single active ingredient is effective against all stages of the flea life cycle.

Controlling fleas is a two-pronged attack. First, the environment needs to be treated; this includes carpets and furniture, especially your Chihuahua's bedding and areas underneath furniture. The environment should be treated with a household spray containing an insect growth regulator and an insecticide to kill the adult fleas. Most insecticides are effective against eggs and larvae; they mimic the fleas' own hormones and stop the eggs and larvae from developing into adult fleas. There are currently no treatments available to attack the pupae stage of the life cycle, so the adult insecticide is used to kill the newly hatched fleas before they find a host. Most insect growth regulators are active for many months, while adult insecticides are only active for a few days.

When treating with a household spray, vacuum before applying the product. This stimulates as many pupae as possible to hatch into adult fleas. The vacuum cleaner should also be treated with an insecticide to prevent the eggs and larvae that have been collected in the vacuum bag from hatching.

climates. They don't bite like fleas; they harpoon. They dig their sharp *proboscis* (nose) into your Chi's skin and drink the blood, which is their only food and drink. Ticks are controlled the same way fleas are controlled.

The American dog tick, *Dermacentor variabilis*, may be the most common dog tick in many areas, especially those areas where the climate is hot and humid. Most dog ticks have life expectancies of a week to six months, depending on climactic conditions. They can neither jump nor fly, but they can crawl slowly and can travel up to 16 feet to reach a sleeping or unsuspecting dog.

The second treatment stage is to apply an adult insecticide to your Chihuahua. Traditionally, this would be in the form of a flea collar or a spray, but more recent innovations include digestible insecticides that poison the fleas when they ingest the dog's blood. There are also drops that, when placed on the back of the dog's neck, spread throughout the hair and skin to kill adult fleas.

Ticks: Though not as common as fleas, ticks are found in tropical and temperate

Mites: Just as fleas and ticks can be problematic for your dog, mites can also lead to an itch fit. Microscopic in size, mites are related to ticks and generally take up permanent residence on their host animal — in this case, your Chihuahua! The term "mange" refers to any infestation caused by one of the mighty mites, of which there are six varieties that smart dog owners should know about.

Roundworms can affect young puppies.

* The *Cheyletiellosis* mite is the hook-mouthed culprit associated with "walking dandruff," a condition that affects dogs as well as cats and rabbits. If untreated, this mange can affect a whole kennel of dogs and can be spread to humans, as well.

* The *Sarcoptes* mite causes intense itching on the dog in the form of a condition known as scabies or sarcoptic mange. Scabies is highly contagious and can be passed to humans. Sometimes an allergic reaction to the mite worsens the severe itching associated with sarcoptic mange.

* Ear mites, *Otodectes cynotis*, lead to otodectic mange, which commonly affects the outer ear canal of the dog, though other areas can be affected as well. Your vet can prescribe a treatment to flush out the ears and kill any eggs in the ears. A month of treatment is necessary to cure mange.

* Two other mites, that are less common in dogs, include *Dermanyssus gallinae* (the "poultry" or "red mite") and *Eutrombicula alfreddugesi* (the North American mite associated with *trombiculidiasis* or chigger infestation). The types of mange caused by both of these mites must be treated by vets.

INTERNAL PARASITES

Most animals — fish, birds, and mammals, including dogs and humans — have worms and other parasites living inside their bodies. According to Dr. Herbert R. Axelrod, a fish pathologist, there are two kinds of parasites: smart and dumb. The "smart" parasites live in peaceful cooperation with their hosts (symbiosis), while the "dumb" parasites kill their hosts. Most worm infections are relatively easy to control. If they are not controlled, they weaken the host dog to the point that other medical problems occur, but they do not kill the host as "dumb" parasites would.

Fleas aren't just an outdoor, summer problem anymore. They can infest your dog and home any time of the year or in any location.

Roundworms: Roundworms that infect dogs live in the dog's intestines and shed eggs continually. It has been estimated that a dog produces about six or more ounces of feces every day, and each ounce averages hundreds of thousands of roundworm eggs. There are no known areas in which dogs roam that do not contain roundworm eggs. Because roundworms infect people too, it is wise to have your dog regularly tested.

Roundworm infection can kill puppies and cause severe problems in adult dogs, as the hatched larvae travel to the lungs and trachea through the bloodstream. Cleanliness is the best prevention against roundworms. Always pick up after your dog and dispose of feces in appropriate receptacles.

Hookworms: Hookworms are dangerous to humans as well as to dogs and cats, and they can be the cause of severe iron-deficiency anemia. The worm uses its teeth to attach itself to the dog's intestines and changes the site of its attachment about six times per day. Each time the worm repositions itself, the dog loses blood and can become anemic.

Symptoms of hookworm infection include dark stools, weight loss, general weakness, pale coloration and anemia as well as possible skin problems. Fortunately, hookworms are easily purged with a number of medications that have proven effective; discuss these with your veterinarian. Most heartworm preventives also include a hookworm insecticide.

Humans, can be infected by hookworms through exposure to contaminated feces. Because the worms cannot complete their life cycle in a human, the worms simply infest the skin and cause irritation. As a preventive, use disposable gloves or a poop-scoop to pick up your dog's droppings. In addition, be sure to prevent your dog (or neighborhood cats) from defecating in children's play areas.

Tapeworms: There are many species of tapeworm, all of which are carried by fleas. Fleas are so small that your Chihuahua could pass them onto your hands, your plate or your food, making it possible for you to ingest a flea that is carrying tapeworm eggs. While tapeworm infection is not life-threatening in dogs (a smart parasite), it can be the cause of a very serious liver disease in humans.

Whipworms: In North America, whipworms are counted among the most common parasitic worms in dogs. Affected dogs may only experience upset stomachs, colic and diarrhea. These worms, however, can live for months or years in the dog, beginning their larval stage in the small intestine, spending their adult stage in the large intestine and finally passing infective eggs through the dog's feces. The only way to detect whipworms is through a fecal examination, though this is not always foolproof. Treatment for whipworms is tricky, due to the worms' unusual life cycle, and often dogs are reinfected due to infective eggs on the ground. Cleaning up droppings in your backyard and in public places is absolutely essential for sanitation purposes and the health of your dog and others.

Threadworms: Though less common than roundworms, hookworms and previously mentioned parasites, threadworms concern dog owners in the southwestern United States and Gulf Coast area where it is hot and humid.

They live in the small intestine of the dog, and measure a mere two millimeters. Like the whipworm, the threadworm's life cycle is very complex, and the eggs and larvae are passed through the feces.

A deadly disease in humans, threadworms readily infect people, mostly through the direct handling of dog feces. Threadworms are most often seen in puppies. Common symptoms include bloody diarrhea and pneumonia. Sick puppies must be isolated and treated immediately; vets recommend a follow-up treatment one month later.

Heartworms: Heartworms are thin, extended worms up to 12 inches long, that live in a dog's heart and the major blood vessels surrounding it. Dogs may have up to 200 heartworms. Symptoms include loss of energy, loss of appetite, coughing, the development of a pot belly and anemia.

Heartworms are transmitted by mosquitoes, which drink the blood of infected dogs and take in larvae with the blood.

After an outdoor outing, be sure to check your Chi for fleas and ticks.

The larvae, called microfilariae, develop within the body of the mosquito and are passed on to the next dog bitten after the larvae mature. It takes two to three weeks for the larvae to develop to the infective stage within the body of the mosquito. Dogs are usually treated at about 6 weeks of age and maintained on a prophylactic dose given monthly.

Blood testing for heartworms is not necessarily indicative of how seriously your dog is infected. Although this is a dangerous disease, it is not easy for a dog to become infected. Discuss the various preventive treatments with your vet, because there are many different types now available. Together you can decide on a safe course of prevention for your dog.

You have probably heard it a thousand times: You are what you eat. Believe it or not, it is very true especially for dogs. Dogs are what you feed them because they have little choice in the matter. Even smart Chihuahua owners, who truly want to feed their dogs the best, often cannot do so because they don't know which foods are best for their dog.

BASIC TYPES

Dog foods are produced in various types: dry, wet (canned), semimoist and frozen.

Dry food is useful for the cost-conscious owner because it tends to be less expensive than others. This food also contains the least fat and the most preservatives. Dry food is bulky and takes longer to eat than other foods, so it's more filling.

Wet food — available in cans or foil pouches — is usually 60 to 70 percent water and is more expensive than dry food. A palatable source of concentrated nutrition, wet food also makes an excellent supplement for underweight dogs or those recovering from an illness. Some smart owners add a little wet food to dry to increase its appeal. Dogs gobble up this savory mixture.

it's a **Fact** Bones can cause gastrointestinal obstruction and perforation and may be contaminated with salmonella or E. coli. Leave them in the trash and give your dog a toy bone instead.

Semimoist food is flavorful but usually contains lots of sugar, which can lead to dental problems and obesity. It's not a good choice for your dog's main diet.

Frozen food, which is available in cooked and raw forms, is usually more expensive than wet food. The advantages of frozen food are similar to those of wet food.

Some manufacturers have developed special foods for small dogs. Some of these contain slightly more protein, fat and calories than standard foods. Manufacturers contend that small dogs need these additional nutrients to fuel their active lifestyle and revved-up metabolism. In reality, your Chihuahua may or may not need them; the nutritional needs of dogs vary considerably, even within the same breed. It's OK to feed your Chi small-breed food, but standard food will provide balanced nutrition, too, as long as you feed appropriate amounts tailored to your buddy's needs.

Some dry foods for small dogs have compositions that are identical to those for larger dogs, but the kibble is smaller to make it easier to chew. Small dogs don't really need smaller kibble, though your dog may prefer it. Many small dogs eat standard-size kibble with no trouble at all.

The amount of food your toy dog needs depends on a number of factors, such as age, activity level, food quality, reproductive status and size. What's the easiest way to figure it out? Start with the manufacturer's recommended amount, and adjust it according to your dog's response. For example, if you feed the recommended amount for a few weeks and your Chihuahua loses weight, increase the amount by 10 to 20 percent. If your dog gains weight, decrease the amount. It won't take long to determine the amount of food that keeps your little friend in optimal condition.

NUTRITION 101

All Chihuahuas (and every breed, for that matter) need proteins, carbohydrates, fats, vitamins and minerals for their optimal growth and health.

■ **Proteins** are used for growth and the repair of muscles, bones and other bodily tissues. They're also used for the production of antibodies, enzymes and hormones. All dogs need protein, but it's especially important for puppies because they grow so rapidly.

Protein sources in dog food include various types of meats, meat meal, meat by-products, eggs and dairy products.

■ **Carbohydrates** are metabolized into glucose, the body's energy source. Carbohydrates are available as sugars, starches and fiber.

Believe it or not, during your Chihuahua's lifetime, you'll buy a few thousand pounds of dog food! Go to **DogChannel.com/Club-Chi** and download a chart that outlines the cost of dog food.

◆ Sugars (simple carbohydrates) are not suitable nutrient sources for dogs.

◆ Starch — a preferred type of carbohydrate in dog food — is found in a variety of plant products. Starches must be cooked in order to be digested.

◆ Fiber (cellulose) — also a preferred type of carbohydrates in dog food — isn't digestible, but it helps the digestive tract function properly.

■ **Fats** are also required for energy and play an important role in skin and coat health, hormone production, nervous system function and vitamin transport. Fat increases the palatability and the calorie count, which can contribute to serious health problems, such as obesity, for puppies or dogs who are allowed to overindulge. Some foods contain added amounts of omega fatty acids such as docosohexaenoic acid, a compound that may enhance brain development and learning in Chi puppies but is not considered an essential nutrient by the Association of American Feed Control Officials (www.aafco.org). Fats used in dog foods include tallow, lard, poultry fat, fish oil and vegetable oils.

■ **Vitamins** and **minerals** participate in muscle and nerve function, bone growth, healing, metabolism and fluid balance. Especially important for your puppy are calcium, phosphorus and vitamin D, which must be supplied in the right balance to ensure proper bone and teeth development.

Just as your dog needs proper nutrition from his food, **water** is an essential nutrient, as well. Water keeps a dog's body properly hydrated and promotes normal body system function. During housetraining, it is necessary to keep an eye on how much water your Chihuahua is drinking, but once he is reliably trained, he should have access to clean, fresh water at all times, especially if you feed him dry food. Make sure that the dog's water bowl is clean, and change the water often.

CHECK OUT THE LABEL

To help you get a feel for what you are feeding your dog, start by taking a look at the nutrition labels. Look for the words "complete and balanced." This tells you that the food meets specific nutritional requirements set by the AAFCO for either adults ("maintenance") or puppies and pregnant/lactating females ("growth and reproduction"). The label must state the group for which it is intended. If you're feeding a puppy, choose a "growth and reproduction" food.

Dogs of all ages love treats and table food, but these goodies can unbalance your Chihuahua's diet and lead to a weight problem if you don't choose and feed them wisely. Table food, whether fed as a treat or as part of a meal, should not account for more than 10 percent of your dog's daily caloric intake. If you plan to give your Chihuahua treats, be sure to include "treat calories" when calculating the daily food requirement, so you don't end up with a pudgy pup!

When shopping for packaged treats, look for ones that provide complete nutrition. They're basically dog food in a fun form. Choose crunchy goodies for chewing fun and dental health. Other ideas for tasty treats include:

✓ small chunks of cooked, lean meat
✓ dry dog food morsels
✓ cheese
✓ veggies (cooked, raw or frozen)
✓ breads, crackers or dry cereal
✓ unsalted, unbuttered, plain, popped popcorn

Some foods, however, can be dangerous or even deadly to your dog. The following can cause digestive upset (vomiting or diarrhea) or toxic reactions that could be fatal:

✗ **avocados:** can cause gastrointestinal irritation, with vomiting and diarrhea, if eaten in sufficient quantity

✗ **baby food:** may contain onion powder; does not provide balanced nutrition for a dog or pup

✗ **chocolate:** contains methylxanthines and theobromine, caffeine-like compounds that can cause vomiting, diarrhea, heart abnormalities, tremors, seizures and even death.

Darker chocolates contain higher levels of the toxic compounds.

✗ **eggs, raw:** whites contain an enzyme that prevents uptake of biotin, a B vitamin; may contain salmonella

✗ **garlic (and related foods):** can cause gastrointestinal irritation and anemia if eaten in sufficient quantity

✗ **grapes/raisins:** can cause kidney failure if eaten in sufficient quantity (the toxic dose varies from dog to dog)

✗ **macadamia nuts:** can cause vomiting, weakness, lack of coordination and other problems

✗ **meat, raw:** may contain harmful bacteria such as salmonella or E. coli

✗ **milk:** can cause diarrhea in some puppies

✗ **onions (and related foods):** can cause gastrointestinal irritation and anemia if eaten in sufficient quantity

✗ **yeast bread dough:** can rise in the gastrointestinal tract, causing obstruction; produces alcohol as it rises

The nutritional analysis refers to crude protein and crude fat — amounts determined in the laboratory. This analysis is technically accurate, but it does not tell you anything about digestibility — how much of the particular nutrient your Chihuahua can actually use. For information about digestibility, contact the manufacturer (check the label for a phone number and website).

Virtually all commercial puppy foods exceed the AAFCO's minimal requirements for protein and fat, the two nutrients most commonly evaluated when comparing foods. Protein levels in dry puppy foods usually range from about 26 to 30 percent; for canned foods, about 9 to 13 percent. The fat content of dry puppy foods is about 20 percent or more; for canned foods, 8 percent or more. Dry food values are larger than canned food values because dry food contains less water; the values are similar when compared on a dry matter basis.

The label also includes a nutritional analysis, which lists minimum protein, minimum fat, maximum fiber and maximum moisture content, as well as other information. (You won't find carbohydrate content because it's everything that isn't protein, fat, fiber and moisture.)

Finally, check the label ingredients, listed in descending order by weight. Manufacturers are allowed to list separately different forms of a single ingredient (e.g., ground corn and corn gluten meal). The food may contain things like meat by-products, meat, bone meal and animal fat, which don't sound appealing but are nutritious and safe for a dog. Higher quality foods have meat or meat products near the top of the list, but you don't need to worry about grain products as long as the label indicates that the food is nutritionally complete. Dogs are omnivores (not carnivores, as commonly believed), so all balanced dog foods contain animal and plant ingredients.

Did You Know?

If you're feeding a puppy food that's complete and balanced, your Chihuahua youngster does not need any dietary supplements such as vitamins, minerals, or other types of food. Dietary supplementation could even harm your puppy by unbalancing her diet. If you have questions about supplementing your Chihuahua's diet, consult your veterinarian.

Feeding your dog is part of your daily routine. Take a break, and have some online fun by playing "Feed the Chihuahua," an exclusive game found only on **DogChannel.com/Club-Chi** — just click on "Games."

SMART TIP!

How can you tell if your Chihuahua is fit or fat? When you run your hands down your pal's sides from front to back, you should be able to easily feel her ribs. It's OK if you feel a little body fat (and, of course, of hair), but you should not feel huge fat pads. You should also be able to feel your Chihuahua's waist — an indentation behind her ribs.

STAGES OF LIFE

When selecting your dog's diet, three stages of development must be considered: the puppy stage, the adult stage and the senior stage.

Puppy Diets: Pups instinctively want to nurse, and a normal puppy will exhibit this behavior from just a few moments following birth. Puppies should be allowed to nurse for about the first six weeks, although from the third or fourth week, the breeder will begin to introduce small portions of suitable solid food. Most breeders like to introduce alternate milk and meat meals initially, building up to weaning time.

By the time puppies are 7 to 8 weeks old, they should be fully weaned and fed solely a proprietary puppy food. Selection of the most suitable, good-quality diet at this time is essential, for a puppy's fastest growth rate is during the first year of his life. Seek advice about your dog's food from your veterinarian. The frequency of meals will be reduced over time, and when a young dog has reached about 10 to 12 months of age, he should be switched to an adult diet.

Puppy and junior diets can be balanced for the needs of your Chihuahua so, except in certain circumstances, additional vitamins, minerals and proteins will not be required.

How many times a day does your Chihuahua need to eat? Puppies — especially toy breeds — have small stomachs and high metabolic rates, so they need to eat several times a day in order to consume sufficient nutrients. If your puppy is younger than 3 months old, feed him four or five meals a day. When your little buddy is 3 to 5 months old, decrease the number of meals to three or four. At 6 months of age, most puppies can move to an adult schedule of two meals a day. If your Chi is prone to hypoglycemia (low blood sugar), a veterinarian may recommend more frequent meals.

Adult Diets: A dog is considered an adult when he has stopped growing. Rely on your veterinarian or canine dietary specialist to recommend an acceptable maintenance diet for your dog. Major dog food manufacturers specialize in this type of food, and smart owners must select the

HYPOGLYCEMIA HELP

Hypoglycemia (low blood sugar) is a potentially life-threatening problem for Chihuahuas and other toy breeds. The most common type of hypoglycemia occurs in pups younger than four months of age. Puppies typically develop hypoglycemia after exercising vigorously, when they're stressed (such as during a trip to the veterinarian) or when they've gone too long without eating.

Toy breed puppies have various anatomical, physiological and behavioral factors that contribute to the development of hypoglycemia: small muscle mass and liver (where glucose is stored as glycogen, a large molecule made up of many glucose molecules), proportionately large brain (a major user of glucose) and high activity level. Immaturity of the body's systems at processing and storing glucose may also play a role.

Early symptoms — trembling, listlessness, incoordination and a dazed or confused demeanor — occur when the brain is deprived of glucose, its sole energy supply. If untreated, hypoglycemia can lead to seizures, collapse, loss of consciousness and death. If your Chihuahua develops symptoms of hypoglycemia, start treatment immediately. Wrap your little buddy in a towel or blanket to keep her warm (shivering makes the hypoglycemia worse). If your Chihuahua is conscious, slowly dribble a little corn syrup or honey into her mouth or give her a dollop of high-calorie dietary-supplement paste (available from your veterinarian). Repeat after 10 minutes, if necessary.

Feed your Chi puppy as soon as she's alert enough to eat. If hypoglycemia causes your Chihuahua to lose consciousness, rub the syrup or paste on her gums and tongue, then immediately take her to the veterinarian for further care. If your puppy is prone to developing hypoglycemia, you should feed her a high-quality nutritionally balanced food four to five times a day.

Healthy high-calorie snacks may help prevent hypoglycemia between meals. If possible, avoid subjecting your Chi puppy to circumstances that may elicit hypoglycemia, such as stressful situations or extended periods of vigorous activity. Most pups outgrow hypoglycemia by the time they're 4 months old.

Consult your veterinarian if your dog continues to have hypoglycemic episodes after this age.

one best suited to their dogs' needs. Do not leave food out all day for "free-choice" feeding, as this freedom inevitably translates to inches around your dog's waist.

Senior Diets: As dogs get older, their metabolism changes. An older dog usually exercises less, moves more slowly and sleeps more. This change in lifestyle and physiological performance requires a change in diet. Because these changes take place slowly, they might not be immediately recognized. These metabolic changes increase the tendency toward obesity, requiring an even more vigilant approach to feeding. Obesity in an older dog compounds the health problems that already accompany old age.

As your Chi gets older, few of his organs will function up to par. His kidneys will slow down and his intestines will become less efficient. These age-related factors are best handled with a change in diet and feeding schedule to give smaller portions that are more easily digested.

Did You Know? Because semimoist food contains lots of sugar, it isn't a good selection for your Chihuahua's main menu. However, it is great as a yummy snack for a toy dog. Try forming the food into little meatballs for a once-a-week treat! She'll love ya for it!

There is not one diet that will be best for every senior Chihuahua. While many elderly Chis will do perfectly fine on lighter or senior diets, other dogs will do better on special premium diets such as lamb and rice. A smart Chihuahua owner will be prudent and sensitive to his or her senior Chihuahua's diet, and this will help control other health complications that may arise with their aging friend. Just keep in mind: Your dog is what he eats!

These delicious, dog-friendly recipes will have your furry friend smacking his lips and salivating for more. Just remember: Treats aren't meant to replace your dog's regular meals. Give your Chihuahua snacks sparingly and continue to feed her nutritious, well-balanced meals.

Cheddar Squares

$1/3$ cup all-natural applesauce
$1/3$ cup low-fat cheddar cheese, shredded
$1/3$ cup water
2 cups unbleached white flour

In a medium bowl, mix all wet ingredients. In a large bowl, mix the flour and cheese. Slowly add the wet ingredients to the flour.

Mix well. Pour batter into a greased 13x9x2-inch pan. Bake at 375-degrees Fahrenheit for 25 to 30 minutes. Bars are done when a toothpick inserted in the center and removed comes out clean. Cool and cut into bars. Makes about 54, $1 1/2$-inch bars.

Peanut Butter Bites

3 tablespoons vegetable oil
$1/4$ cup smooth peanut butter, no salt or sugar
$1/4$ cup honey
$1 1/2$ teaspoons baking powder
2 eggs
2 cups whole wheat flour

In a large bowl, mix all ingredients until dough is firm. If the dough is too sticky, mix in a small amount of flour. Knead dough on a lightly floured surface until firm. Roll out dough until it is half an inch thick and cut with cookie cutters. Put cookies on a cookie sheet half an inch apart. Bake at 350-degrees Fahrenheit for 20 to 25 minutes. When done, cookies should be firm to the touch. Remove cookies from the oven, and leave cookies for one to two hours to harden. Makes about 40, 2-inch-long cookies.

No matter what the television commercial models with long, flowing tresses tell you, the ingredients you add externally to your dog's hair will not change a brittle, lifeless coat into a soft, healthy coat. The truth is that if you want your Chihuahua to have a healthy coat, you need to take a close look at your dog's nutrition. Healthy hair and skin begins with good nutrition.

A good premium dog food is the best place to start growing a healthy coat. Your toy dog's diet is not the place to economize. Purchase the best food you can afford and resist the impulse to save money at your Chihuahua's expense. Chihuahua skin can be sensitive, so consult your veterinarian when choosing your dog's food. Once you've established a good nutritional basis, you can move on to improving the coat from the outside.

GROOMING TOOLS

Smooth and long-coated Chihuahuas don't require much in the way of special tools. Although your dog may look like he doesn't need to be brushed, Chihuahuas do shed. If you don't want to spend an hour picking your dog's coat off your suit, then spend a few minutes every other day running the brush over his body. Here are the recommend tools you'll need to keep your Chihuahua looking well groomed.

- a rubber slicker brush. This is a square, flat brush with pin-like teeth.
- a soft bristle brush
- a medium-toothed comb. This is useful for grooming long-coated Chihuahuas to remove knots and matted hair.

● a chamois grooming glove. This handy extra for smooth Chi puppies gives their coat a nice sheen.

● a soft face cloth for wiping the face

● cotton balls to clean your pup's ears

● styptic powder. It's used to stop bleeding if you accidentally clip a nail too short and nip the quick. Ordinary cake flour will work well, too.

● a pair of nail clippers and a nail file

● nonslip rubber mat. Available in the kitchenware department of most supermarkets, put it in the bath or sink and on your grooming surface to provide a nice, secure surface for your puppy to stand on.

● a hair dryer. For a long-coated Chi puppy, consider purchasing a hair-dryer that's specialized for pets. Never use your own hair dryer, as even the lowest setting can be too harsh for your puppy's skin. You also can find pet hair dryers that clip onto countertops, which will allow you to use both hands when brushing your Chihuahua puppy's coat.

Use a box or basket to store the tools. Keeping your grooming equipment organ-

NOTABLE & QUOTABLE

After removing a tick, clean your dog's skin with hydro-gen peroxide. If Lyme disease is common where you live, have your veterinarian test the tick. Tick preventative medication will discourage ticks from attaching and kill any that do.

— groomer Andrea Vilardi from West Paterson, N.J.

It's a good idea to introduce a grooming routine to your Chihuahua pup soon after you bring her home, so that she will learn to enjoy hands-on attention and look forward to spending quality time with you.

ized will come in handy when your little darling finds things in the yard to roll in and desperately needs a deodorizing bath or when you cut the nail back too far. Have the styptic powder close at hand so you aren't searching for it while your dog's paw oozes blood. Your third-grade teacher was right: Being organized saves time!

These supplies can readily be found in any well-stocked pet store. If you have questions about the type of shampoos to purchase, ask your breeder, veterinarian or the pet professionals working in the store.

BATHING MADE SIMPLE

Lucky, lucky you. Not only did you show great wisdom in selecting the super lightweight model, but your breed comes in two coat types, smooth and long-coated, both of which are easy to maintain. Try not to look too smug as you pass the Lhasa Apso owner's shopping cart, which is stocked with every detangling product available in the store!

Because of his small size, you have the choice of bathing your Chihuahua in the kitchen sink or in the bathtub. Of the two, the sink is the better choice. Not only will your knees thank you when you don't have to kneel on the hard bathroom tile, but your back will too because Chihuahuas are so small you have to bend down farther than you might like to shampoo them. Try putting a small rubber bathmat in the sink to give your dog a firm, non-slippery support. You'll also want to put the drain stopper in, loosened, so water can drain away. You can use a hose attachment if you have one, but if not, you can rinse your Chi with a plastic cup.

Prior to wetting the coat, take a moment to block each ear with a cot-

Regularly brushing your Chi's hair will distribute the natural oils in it, making it shinier.

ton ball. This will help prevent water from draining into the ear canal. Begin applying the shampoo around the neck and work back toward the tail. Pay attention to your dog's body, looking for new bumps or growths. Smart owners who regularly bathe their pet will notice new changes to their Chi's physique and can contact their veterinarians as soon as problems arise.

Massage the shampoo into the coat, under the tail and even in the pads of the paw. Put a small amount of shampoo on your hand or a washcloth and carefully distribute it on the head.

Rinsing the coat is as important as the actual shampooing. When you rinse your Chihuahua, pay attention to his belly, genitals and feet. Soap residue left on your dog can cause dry skin, flaking and itching. Rinse the coat until it feels squeaky clean. If you are using a coat conditioner, apply it at this time, and once again rinse, rinse and rinse some more.

Remove the cotton balls from the ears. Wrap your Chi in a big fluffy towel and gently rub to remove the water. Use a hair dryer so your Chi doesn't become chilled by air drying. Test the air flow against your wrist; if it feels too warm, turn down the heat setting. You don't want to burn your dog's delicate skin. Dry your dog completely before setting him down.

TOOTH TRUTH

Many small breeds have real challenges with their dental health, and Chihuahuas

JOIN OUR ONLINE Club Chi™

Every Chihuahua should look chic. What do you need to keep your dog looking his best? Go to Club Chi (**DogChannel.com/ Club-Chi**) and download a checklist of essential grooming equipment you and your toy dog will need.

are no exception. "You should teach your Chihuahua to let you brush his teeth with a soft toothbrush and toothpaste made for dogs," says Peggy Wilson, the former president of the Chihuahua Club of America. "You can even clean the teeth by wrapping a piece of gauze around your finger."

When plaque coats the teeth, it begins to harden into tartar. The hard coating creeps under the gum line creating pockets beneath the gums where bacteria thrive. In time, your Chihuahua can develop gingivitis (the first stage of gum disease, characterized by inflammation) and tooth loss. However, the real threat to your dog's health comes from the bacteria in the pockets under the gums. The bacteria can be absorbed into the bloodstream and travel to the major organs of the body, such

SMART TIP!

The family pet shouldn't be the center of a power struggle between children and parents. Divvy up grooming responsibilities early on, and make the issue non-negotiable. A clean toy dog is welcomed into the house with the family; a dirty one is banished to the backyard, doomed to be on the outside looking in.

as the heart, causing infection.

Begin to train your Chihuahua to accept tooth brushing by quietly sitting on the sofa and holding him on your lap. The first couple of days, just insert your finger into your dog's mouth and massage the gums along the outside. Praise and reward your dog like crazy when he accepts this calmly. Once

Make bath time fun with yummy treats and fun toys.

your dog accepts this massage, wrap a piece of gauze around your finger and gently massage the gums and teeth. Add toothpaste to the gauze and again massage the gums. (No sharing your toothpaste; your dog will appreciate the flavorings added to his doggie variety). Generally, you don't need to worry about the interior of the mouth. Hard kibble and the tongue help to keep the plaque from building up there. Finally, graduate to a soft toothbrush with toothpaste. Try to brush the teeth on a regular schedule of two to three times a week.

NAIL 4-1-1

Immediately after the bath is the best time to clip the nails because the water has softened the nails and your Chi may be somewhat tired-out by the bath. Nail trimming is recommended every two weeks with nail clippers or a nail grinding tool. Short nails are crucial to maintaining the breed's normal foot shape. Long nails will permanently damage any dog's feet, but the tight ligaments of round, arched feet will break down more quickly. If your dog's nails are clicking on the floor, they need trimming.

Your toy dog should be accustomed to having his nails trimmed at an early age, because it will be part of your maintenance routine throughout his life. Not only does it look nicer, but long nails can scratch some-

one unintentionally. Also, a long nail has a better chance of ripping and bleeding, or causing the feet to spread.

Before you start cutting, make sure you can identify the "quick" (the vein in the center of each nail). It will bleed if accidentally cut, which will be quite painful for the dog as it contains nerve endings. Keep some type of clotting agent on hand, such as a styptic pencil or styptic powder (the type used for shaving). This will stop the bleeding quickly when applied to the end of the cut nail. Do not panic if this happens, just stop the bleeding and talk soothingly to your dog. Once he has calmed down, move on to the next nail. It is better to clip a little at a time, particularly with dogs who have darker-colored nails.

Hold your pup steady as you begin trimming his nails; you do not want him to make any sudden movements or run away. Talk to him soothingly and stroke him as you clip. Holding his foot in your hand, simply take off the end of each nail in one quick clip. You can purchase nail clippers that are specially made for dogs; you can probably find them wherever you buy grooming supplies.

Watch out for the quick when cutting nails.

Don't think of grooming sessions as chores; think of them as great bonding time with your Chihuahua.

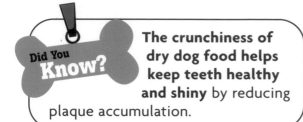

Did You Know? The crunchiness of dry dog food helps keep teeth healthy and shiny by reducing plaque accumulation.

There are two predominant types of clippers. One is the guillotine clipper, which is a hole with a blade in the middle. Squeeze the handles, and the blade meets the nail and chops it off. Sounds gruesome, and for some dogs, it is intolerable. Scissor-type clippers are gentler on the nail. The important thing to make sure of is that the blades on either of these clippers are sharp. Once you are at the desired length, use a nail file to smooth the rough edges of the nails so they don't catch on carpeting or debris outdoors.

When grinding, use a low speed (5,000 to 10,000 rpm) cordless nail grinder fitted with a fine grade (100 grit) sandpaper cylinder. Stone cylinders are more prone to heat buildup and vibration. Hold the dog's paw firmly in one hand spreading the toes slightly apart. Touch the spinning grinder wheel to the nail tip for one or two seconds without applying pressure. Repeat if necessary to remove only the nail tip protruding beyond the quick. Grinders have the added benefit of leaving nails smooth and free of sharp, jagged edges produced by traditional nail clippers.

If the procedure becomes more than you can deal with, just remember: Groomers and veterinarians charge a nominal fee to clip nails. By using their services you won't have to see your pet glower at you for the rest of the night.

When inspecting feet, you must check not only the nails but also the pads of the feet. Take care that the pads have not become cracked and always check between the pads to be sure that nothing has become lodged there. Depending upon the season, there may be a danger of grass seeds or thorns becoming embedded, or even tar from the road getting stuck. Butter, by the way, is useful to help remove tar from his feet.

SIMPLE EAR CLEANING

Although Chihuahuas have those cute upright ears, they still need to be cleaned regularly. Wilson wraps a cotton ball around one finger and gently wipes out the ear. Do not insert anything into the ear canal; only clean the outer visible section of the ear. Healthy ears are light pink in color and shouldn't have any odor. If your Chihuahua has red or swollen ears, or a foul-smelling fluid exuding from the canal, it needs to see the veterinarian.

Commercial ear cleaners can be purchased at pet-supply stores. Use a clean cotton ball for each ear, because if the dog has an ear infection it can be transferred to the healthy ear by using the same swab for both ears.

GROOMING LONG-COATED CHIS

Although the long-coated Chihuahua may have more coat than the smooth variety, he's still fairly easy to groom. "There isn't much in the way of grooming besides routine brushing, and a little bit of neatening up," Wilson says. "For show dogs, trim the hair between their pads because they are supposed to have dainty feet. Keep the nails short enough not to impede movement. The floor can be slippery, so shorter nails also allow the foot pads a better grip as they move around the ring."

Any trimming of the rest of the coat is minimal. "The whiskers can either be trimmed or not," Wilson says. "Either is correct, and you may trim a little around the anus, although nothing extreme. The look is

Your Chihuahua will look *muy buena* after you give her a good bath!

Dogs can't rinse and spit after a brushing, so a dog's toothpaste must be safe for her to swallow. Always use a toothpaste specially formulated for dogs when brushing your Chihuahua's teeth.

supposed to be neat, but natural." She adds a little advice for smooth Chihuahua owners: "Smooths have ruffs around their necks. Be sure not to remove this hair."

Wilson suggests that you brush your Chi regularly to keep tangles at a minimum. "Without brushing, long-coated Chihuahuas

Gently swab around your Chi's ears to keep them clean. However, never insert anything into his ear canal.

can tangle behind the elbows, ears and tail," she says. "Use a soft slicker brush to keep the coat untangled. They shed a couple times a year, so you may see coat loss during these times."

Brushing should be done several times a week and followed with the comb. If the comb snags a tangle, try to separate it with your fingers and brush a little more. You are striving for a natural appearance, so haircuts are not necessary for this breed.

FIGHTING FLEA INFESTATIONS

Chihuahuas, like other breeds, can become targets for fleas during the spring and summer months. Because of their small size, a severe flea infestation quickly could become a threat to their health.

One safe method is to use a flea comb each night. Set the dog on your lap and have a cup of water containing a couple of drops of cooking oil nearby. Draw the flea comb through the coat and if a flea pops up with it, lift the flea off the comb surface and deposit it into the water. The oil will coat the flea, and it will die.

With a little training and work, you and your Chihuahua can establish a working routine that keeps him clean and sweet smelling. His coat will sparkle with health, and he will be on the right track for a long and healthy life.

REWARD A JOB WELL DONE

Rewarding your pet for behaving during grooming is the best way to ensure stress free grooming throughout its lifetime. Bathing energizes your pet, and using the time immediately after grooming as play time is the best way to reward your Chi for a job well done. Watching your clean, healthy Chi tear from room to room in sheer joy is your reward for being a caring owner.

Six Tips for Chihuahua Care

1. Grooming tools can be scary to some dogs, so let yours see and sniff everything at the onset. Keep your beauty sessions short, too. Some Chihuahuas won't enjoy standing still for too long.
2. Look at your dog's eyes for any discharge, and his ears for inflammation, debris or foul odor. If you notice anything that doesn't look right, contact your veterinarian ASAP.
3. Choose a time to groom your dog when you don't have to rush, and assemble all of the grooming tools before you begin. This way, you can focus on your dog's needs instead of having to stop in the middle of the session.
4. Start establishing a grooming routine the day after you bring him home. A regular grooming schedule will make it easier to remember what touch-up tasks your dog needs.
5. Proper nail care will help with your dog's gait and spinal alignment. Nails that are too long can force a dog to walk improperly. Also, extra-long nails can snag and tear, causing painful injury to your Chihuahua.
6. Good dental health prevents gum disease and tooth loss. Brush your Chi's teeth two or three times a week, and see a vet yearly.

Six Questions to Ask a Groomer

1. Do you cage dry? Are you willing to hand dry or air dry my pet?
2. What type of shampoo are you using? Is it tearless? If not, do you have a tearless variety available for use?
3. Will you restrain my dog if he acts up for nail clipping? What methods do you use for difficult dogs?
4. Are you familiar with the Chihuahua breed? Do you have any references from other toy dog owners?
5. Is the shop air-conditioned during hot weather?
6. Will my dog be getting brushed or just bathed?

TRAIN

You know the stereotype: The tiny dog nestled in the ample bosom of the wealthy dowager, snapping and snarling at all who come near. His feet never touch the ground, and no one other than his doting owner ever touches him.

What a shame. When given the opportunity, the Chihuahua can be as much a dog as the best of them. It's easy to fall into the trap of thinking your Chihuahua doesn't need training. He's so little; it's no big deal to just pick him up when you need to take him somewhere. But if you want him to be mentally and physically healthy — and to be a well-behaved member of society — you'll need to square your shoulders, and put your Chihuahua back on the floor.

The increasing use of dog-friendly methods is a blessing to all dogs, and especially to toy breeds, which are most vulnerable to injury from heavy-handed training. It doesn't take much of a jerk on a choke chain to damage the trachea of a toy dog. Positive training techniques are basically the same for dogs of all sizes, but you'll encounter special challenges when you're training your tiny Chihuahua.

Did You Know? **The prime period for socialization is short.** Most behavior experts agree that positive experiences during the 10 week period between 1 and 14 weeks of age are vital to the development of a puppy who'll grow into an adult dog with a sound temperament.

LEARNING SOCIAL GRACES

Now that you have done all of the preparatory work and have helped your Chihuahua get accustomed to his new home and family, it's time for a smart owner to have some fun! Socializing your tiny pup will give you the opportunity to show off your new friend, and your toy dog gets to reap the benefits of being an adorable little creature whom people will want to pet and who'll think he is absolutely precious!

Besides getting to know his new family, your puppy should be exposed to other people, animals and situations, but of course, he must not come into close contact with dogs you don't know well until he has had all his vaccinations. This will help him become well-adjusted as he grows up and less prone to being timid or fearful of the new things he will encounter.

Your pup's socialization began at the breeder's home, but now it is your responsibility to continue it. The socialization he receives up until 12 weeks of age is the most critical, as this is the time when he forms his impressions of the outside world. Be especially careful during the 8- to 10-week-old period, also known as the fear period. The interaction he receives during this time should be gentle and reassuring. Lack of socialization can manifest itself as fear and aggression as your dog grows up. Your pup needs lots of human contact, affection, handling and exposure to other animals.

Once your Chihuahua has received his necessary vaccinations, take him out and about (on his leash, of course). Walk him around the neighborhood, take him on errands, let people pet him and let him meet other dogs and pets. Expose your toy dog to different people — men, women, kids, babies, men with beards, teenagers with cell phones or riding skateboards, joggers, shop-

pers, someone in a wheelchair, a pregnant woman, etc. Make sure your Chihuahua explores different surfaces like sidewalks, gravel and a puddle. Positive experiences are the key to building your Chi's confidence. It's up to you to make sure your Chihuahua safely discovers the world so he will be calm, confident and well-socialized.

It's important that you take the lead in all socialization experiences and never put your pup in a scary or potentially harmful situation. Be mindful of your Chihuahua's limitations. Fifteen minutes at a public market is fine; two hours at a loud outdoor concert is too much. Meeting vaccinated, tolerant and gentle older dogs is great. Meeting dogs whom you don't know isn't a good idea, especially if they appear energetic, dominant or fearful. Control the situations in which you place your pup.

The best way to socialize your puppy to a new experience is to make him think it's the best thing ever. You can do this with a lot of happy talk, enthusiasm and, yes, food. To convince your puppy that almost any experience is a blast, always carry treats. Consider carrying two types — a bag of his puppy chow, which you can give him when introducing him to nonthreatening experiences, and a bag of high-value, mouth-watering treats to give him when introducing him to scarier experiences.

TRAINING WITH CLASS

To train a Chihuahua, a smart owner may enroll in an obedience class. There you can teach him good manners as you learn how and why he behaves the way he does. Find out how to communicate with your dog and how to recognize and understand how he communicates with you. Suddenly, your dog will take on a new role in your life; he will be smart, interesting, well-behaved and fun to be with; he will demonstrate his bond of devotion to you daily. In other words, your Chi will do wonders for your ego because he will constantly remind you that you are not only his leader, you are his hero!

Those involved with teaching dog obedience and counseling owners about their dogs' behavior have discovered some interesting facts about dog ownership. Training dogs when they are puppies results in the highest success rate in developing well-mannered and well-adjusted adult dogs. Training an older dog — from 6 months to 6 years of age — can produce almost equal results, providing that a smart owner accepts the dog's slower learning rate and is willing to work patiently to help their dog succeed. Unfortunately, many owners

SMART TIP!

If your toy dog refuses to sit with both haunches squarely beneath her and instead sits on one side or the other, she may have a physical reason for doing so. Discuss the habit with your veterinarian to be certain that your dog isn't suffering from a structural problem.

of untrained adult dogs lack patience, so they do not persist until their dogs are successful at certain behaviors.

Training a Chi puppy aged 10 to 16 weeks (20 weeks at the most) is like working with a dry sponge in a pool of water. The pup soaks up whatever you show him and constantly looks for more things to do and learn.

Treats and praise are both great training rewards. Use them both during your lessons.

it's a Fact

Training works best when blended into daily life. When your toy dog asks for something — food, play or whatever else — cue her to do something for you first. Reward her by granting her request. Practice in different settings, so your Chi will learn to listen regardless of her surroundings.

Don't let your training sessions turn into marathons. Keep them short and interesting for better results.

At this early age, his body is not yet producing hormones; therein is the reason for such a high success rate. Without hormones, he is focused on his owners and not particularly interested in investigating other places, dogs, people, etc. You are his leader: his provider of food, water, shelter and security. He latches onto you and wants to stay close. He will usually follow you from room to room, will not let you out of his sight when you are outdoors with him and will respond in a similar manner to the people and animals you encounter. If you greet a friend warmly, he will be happy to greet the person as well. If, however, you are hesitant, even anxious, about the approach of a stranger, he will respond accordingly.

Once the puppy begins to produce hormones, his natural curiosity emerges and he begins to investigate the world around him. It is at this time when you may notice that the untrained dog begins to wander away from you and even ignore your cues to stay close.

There are usually classes within a reasonable distance of your home, but you also can do a lot to train your dog yourself. Whatever the circumstances, the key to successfully training your Chihuahua without formal obedience classes lies within the pages of this book. This chapter is devoted to helping you train your Chihuahua at home. If the recommended procedures are followed faithfully, you may expect positive results that will prove rewarding to you and your dog.

Whether your new charge is a puppy or a mature adult, the methods of teaching and the techniques used in training basic behaviors are the same. After all, no dog, whether puppy or adult, likes harsh or inhumane methods. All creatures, however, respond favorably to gentle motivational methods and sincere praise and encouragement.

With the proper training, your toy dog will be as well-behaved as she is adorable. One certification that all dogs should receive is the American Kennel Club Canine Good Citizen, which rewards dogs with good manners. Go to **DogChannel.com/Club-Chi** and click on "Downloads" to get the 10 steps required for your dog to be a CGC.

The following behavioral problems are the ones that owners encounter the most. Every dog and situation is unique. Because behavioral abnormalities are the primary reason owners abandon their pets, we hope that you will make a valiant effort to train your Chihuahua from the start.

BASIC CUES

All Chihuahuas, regardless of your training and relationship goals, need to know at least five basic good-manner behaviors: sit, down, stay, come and heel. Here are tips for teaching your dog these important cues.

SIT: Every dog should learn how to sit.
- Hold a tasty treat at the end of your dog's nose.
- Move the treat over his head.
- When your Chihuahua sits, click a clicker or say "Yes!"
- Feed your dog the treat.
- If your dog jumps up, hold the treat lower. If he backs up, back him into a corner and wait until he sits. Be patient. Keep your clicker handy, and click (or say "Yes!") and treat anytime he offers a sit.
- When he easily offers sits, say "sit" just before he offers, so he can make the association between the word and the behavior. Add the sit cue when you know you can get the behavior. Your dog doesn't know what the word means until you repeatedly associate it with the appropriate behavior.
- When your Chihuahua sits easily on cue, start using intermittent reinforcement by clicking some sits but not others. At first, click most sits and skip an occasional one (this is a high rate of reinforcement). Gradually make your clicks more and more random.

DOWN: If your Chihuahua can sit, then he can learn to lie down.

◆ Have your Chihuahua sit.
◆ Hold the treat in front of his nose. Move it down slowly, straight toward the floor (toward his toes). If he follows all the way down, click and treat.
◆ If he gets stuck, slowly move the treat down. Click and treat for small movements downward — moving his head a bit lower or inching one paw forward. Keep clicking and treating until your Chihuahua is all the way down. This is called "shaping" — rewarding small pieces of a behavior until your dog succeeds.
◆ If your dog stands as you move the treat toward the floor, have him sit and move the treat more slowly downward, shaping with clicks and treats for small movements down as long as he is sitting. If he stands, cheerfully say "Oops!" (which means "Sorry, no treat for that!"), have him sit and try again.
◆ If shaping isn't working, sit on the floor with your knee raised. Have your Chihuahua sit next to you. Put your hand with the treat under your knee and lure him under your leg so that he lies down and crawls to follow the treat. Click and treat!
◆ When you can lure the down easily, add the verbal cue, wait a few seconds to let your dog think, then lure him down to show him the association. Repeat until he'll go down on the verbal cue. Then begin using intermittent reinforcement.

STAY: What good are sit and down cues if your dog doesn't stay?
▲ Start with your Chihuahua in a sit or down position.
▲ Put the treat in front of your dog's nose and keep it there.
▲ Click and reward several times while he is in position, then release him with a cue that you will always use to tell him the stay is over. Common release cues are: "all done," "break," "free," "free dog," "at ease" and "OK."

▲ When your Chihuahua will stay in a sit or down position while you click and treat, add your verbal stay cue. Say "stay," pause for a second or two, click and say "stay" again. Release.

▲ When your Chi is getting the idea, say "stay," whisk the treat out of sight behind your back, click and whisk the treat back. Be sure to get it all the way to his nose, so he does not jump up. Gradually increase the duration of the stay.

▲ When your Chi will stay for 15 to 20 seconds, add small distractions: shuffling your feet, moving your arms, small hops, etc. Increase distractions gradually. If he makes mistakes, you're adding too much, too fast.

▲ When he'll stay for 15 to 20 seconds with distractions, gradually add distance.

SMART TIP!

If you begin teaching the heel cue by taking long walks and letting the dog pull you along, she may misinterpret this action as an acceptable form of taking a walk. When you pull back on the leash to counteract her pulling, she will read that tug as a signal to pull even harder!

Have your Chi stay, take a half-step back, click, return and treat. When he'll stay with a half-step, tell him to stay, take a full step back, click and return. Always return to treat after you click, but before you release. If you always return, his stay becomes strong. If you call him to you, his stay gets weaker due to his eagerness to come to you.

Try a harness instead of a traditional collar for training or even everyday walks.

COME: A reliable recall — coming when called — can be a challenging behavior to teach. To teach this cue successfully, you need to install an automatic response to your "come" cue — one so automatic that your Chihuahua doesn't even stop to think when he hears it, but will spin on his heels and charge to you at full speed.

■ Start by charging a come cue the same way you charged your clicker. If your Chihuahua already ignores the word "come," pick a different cue, like "front" or "hugs." Say your cue and feed him a bit of scrumptious treat. Repeat this until your toy dog's eyes light up when he hears the cue. Now you're ready to start training.

■ With your Chi on a leash, run away several steps and call out your charged cue. When he follows, click the clicker. Feed him a treat when he reaches you. For a more enthusiastic come, run away at full speed as you call him. When he follows at a gallop, click, stop running and give him a treat. The better your Chihuahua gets at coming, the farther away he can be when you call him.

■ Once your Chihuahua understands the come cue, play with more people, each with a clicker and treats. Stand a short distance apart and take turns calling and running away. Click and treat in turn as he comes to each of you. Gradually increase the distance until he comes flying to each person from greater distances.

■ When you and your Chihuahua are ready to practice in wide-open spaces, attach a long line — a 20- to 50-foot leash — to your dog, so you can gather up your Chi if that taunting butterfly nearby is too much of a temptation. Then, head to a practice area where there are less tempting distractions.

HEEL: Heeling means that your dog walks beside you without pulling. It takes time and patience on your part to succeed at teaching your dog that you will not proceed unless he is walking calmly beside you. Pulling out ahead on the leash is definitely not acceptable.

● Begin by holding the leash in your left hand as your Chihuahua sits beside your left leg. Move the loop end of the leash to your right hand, but keep your left hand short on the leash so it keeps your dog close to you.

● Say "heel" and step forward on your left foot. Keep your Chihuahua close to you and take three steps. Stop and have the dog sit next to you in what is called the heel position. Praise verbally, but do not touch your dog. Hesitate a moment and begin again with "heel," taking three steps and stopping, at which point the dog is told to sit again.

Your goal here is to have your Chihuahua walk those three steps without pulling on the leash. Once he will walk calmly beside you for three steps without pulling, increase the number of steps you take to five. When he will walk politely beside you while you take five steps, you can increase the length of your walk to 10 steps. Keep increasing the

SMART TIP!

Once your Chi understands what behavior goes with a specific cue, it is time to start weaning her off the food treats. At first, give a treat after each exercise. Then, start to give a treat only after every other exercise. Mix up the times when you offer a food reward and when you only offer praise. This way your dog will never know when she is going to receive food and praise or only praise.

NOTABLE & QUOTABLE

Sit on the floor to practice your dog's training exercises. It's less intimidating for her — and easier on your back. Alternatively, set her on a raised surface, such as a tabletop covered with a blanket. Make sure she's comfortable and confident there — if not, go back to the floor.
— *Pat Miller, trainer and owner of the Peaceable Paws dog-training facility in Hagerstown, Md.*

length of your stroll until your toy dog will walk quietly beside you without pulling for as long as you want him to heel. When you stop heeling, indicate to the dog that the exercise is over by petting him and saying "OK, good dog." The "OK" is used as a release word, meaning that the exercise is finished, and he is free to relax.

● If you are dealing with a Chihuahua who insists on pulling, simply put on your brakes and stand your ground until your Chihuahua realizes that the two of you are not going anywhere until he is beside you and moving at your pace, not his. It may take some time just standing there to convince your dog that you are the leader, and you will be the one to decide on the direction and speed of your travel.

● Each time the dog looks up at you or slows down to give a slack leash between the two of you, quietly praise him and say, "Good heel. Good dog." Eventually, your Chihuahua will begin to respond, and within a few days he will be walking politely beside you without pulling on the leash. At first, the training sessions should be kept short and very positive; soon your dog will be able to walk nicely with you for increasingly longer distances. Remember to give your dog free time and the opportunity to run and play when you have finished heel practice.

TRAINING TIPS

If not properly socialized, managed and trained, even a well-bred Chi will exhibit undesirable behaviors such as jumping up, barking, chasing and chewing. You can prevent these annoying habits and help your Chihuahua become the perfect dog you've wished for by following some basic training and behavior guidelines.

Use appropriately-sized equipment. Purchase collars and leashes to scale for your little one. A huge brass buckle is like an anchor for your Chihuahua, and if it smacks him in the face once or twice, he won't be eager to train or go for walks with you. A harness may be a better choice for a Chihuahua than a collar, to avoid any potential damage to the throat.

Move gently. Try to lighten your step and move with gentle purpose when training and interacting with your Chihuahua. You probably outweigh your pup 20 to 30 times., imagine strolling next to a 2,500-pound gargantuan towering over you. Now imagine that gargantuan stomping in heavy boots, barely missing your tiny self with each step. Tread lightly and wear soft-soled shoes.

Use teensy treats. With mid- to large-sized dogs, we feed pea-sized treats. With itty-bitty dogs you need to use rice-grain-sized treats. If your treats are too large your Chihuahua will fill up in no time and your training sessions will be too short.

Keep him safe. Your dog depends on you to be his protector and defender. Don't ever let anyone — your trainer, groomer, veterinarian, friends, family — do anything to him that you aren't comfortable with, and don't let yourself be talked into doing anything against your better judgment. Although it's good for him to play with other dogs to be well-adjusted, larger dogs

Don't show frustration during training sessions; your Chihuahua will pick up on your bad vibes. Be positive, and try again.

can and do present a significant threat to a toy dog's safety. More than one little dog has been killed in the jaws of a big dog. Err on the side of caution when choosing your playmates for your Chi.

Think big. Don't let your Chihuahua's diminutive size impede your training goals. If you want a well-socialized companion who accompanies you everywhere, he's your man. Toy dogs are often allowed places where their larger brothers aren't so socialization is especially important for this breed.

THE THREE-STEP PROGRAM

Perhaps it's too late to give your dog consistency, training and management from the start. Maybe he came from a toy dog rescue or a shelter, or you didn't realize the importance of these rules when he was a pup. He already may have learned some bad behaviors, perhaps they're even part of his genetic package. Many problems can be modified with ease using the following three-step process for changing an unwanted behavior.

STEP NO. 1: Visualize the behavior you want from your dog. If you simply try to stop your Chihuahua from doing something, you leave a behavior vacuum. You need to fill that vacuum with something, so your dog doesn't return to the same behavior or fill it with one that's even worse! If you're tired of your dog jumping up, decide what you'd prefer

JOIN OUR ONLINE **Club Chi**™

The best way to get your toy dog well-socialized is to introduce her to different kinds of people and situations. Go online to download a socialization checklist at **DogChannel.com/Club-Chi**

instead. A dog who greets people by sitting politely in front of them is a joy to own.

STEP NO. 2: Prevent your toy dog from being rewarded for behavior that you don't want. Management to the rescue! When your Chihuahua jumps up to greet you or get your attention, turn your back and step away to show him that jumping up no longer works.

STEP NO. 3: Generously reinforce the desired behavior. Remember, dogs repeat behaviors that reward them. If your Chihuahua no longer gets attention for jumping up and is heavily reinforced with attention and treats for sitting, he will offer sits instead of jumping, because sits get him what he wants.

COUNTER CONDITIONING

Behaviors that respond well to the three-step process are those where a dog does something in order to get good stuff. He jumps up to get attention. He countersurfs because he finds good stuff on the counters. He nips at your hands to get you to play with him.

The three steps don't work well when you're dealing with behaviors that are based in strong emotion, such as aggression and fear, or with hardwired behaviors such as chasing prey. With these, a smart Chi owner can change the emotional or hardwired response through counter conditioning — programming a new emotional or automatic response to the stimulus by giving it a new association. Here's how you would counter condition a Chihuahua who chases after skateboarders when you're walking him on a leash.

1. Have a supply of very high-value treats, such as canned chicken.

2. Station yourself with your dog on a leash at a location where skateboarders will pass by at a subthreshold distance "X" — that is, where your Chihuahua alerts but doesn't lunge and bark.

3. Wait for a skateboarder. The instant your Chi notices the skateboarder, feed him bits of chicken, nonstop, until the skateboarder is gone.

4. Repeat many times until, when the skateboarder appears, your Chihuahua looks at you with a big grin as if to say, "Yay! Where's my chicken?" This is a conditioned emotional response, or CER.

5. When you have a consistent CER at X, decrease the distance slightly, perhaps by 1 foot, and repeat until you consistently get the CER at this distance.

6. Continue decreasing the distance and obtaining a CER at each level, until a skateboarder zooming right past your Chi elicits the happy "Where's my chicken?" response. Now go back to distance X and add a second zooming skateboarder. Continue this process of gradual desensitization until your Chihuahua doesn't turn a hair at a bevy of skateboarders.

LEAVE IT ALONE

Toy dogs enjoy eating, which makes it easy to train using treats. However, some Chis gobble down anything even remotely edible. This could include fresh food, rotten food and any item that's ever been in contact with food. So, if you don't want your Chihuahua gulping trash, teach him to leave things alone when told.

Place a tempting tidbit on the floor and cover it with your hand (gloved against teeth, if necessary). Say your cue word ("Leave it" or "Nah"). Your dog might lick, nibble and paw your hand; don't give in or you reward bad manners.

Wait until your dog moves away, then click or praise and give him a treat. Do not let your dog eat the temptation food that's on the floor, only the treats you give him. Repeat until your dog stops moving toward the food temptation.

Lift your hand momentarily, letting your dog see the temptation. Say the cue word. Be ready to protect the treat but instantly reward your toy dog if he resists temptation. Repeat, moving your hand farther away and waiting longer before clicking and rewarding.

Gradually increase the difficulty — practice in different locations, add new temptations, drop treats from standing height and drop several at a time and step away.

Remember to use your cue word, so your dog will know what he's expected to do. Always reward good behavior! Rehearse this skill daily for a week. After that, you'll have enough real-life opportunities to practice.

it's a **Fact**

Behaviors are best trained by breaking them down into their simplest components, teaching those and then linking them together to end up with the complete behavior. Keep treats small so you can reward many times without stuffing your Chi. Remember, don't bore your toy dog; avoid excessive repetition.

JOIN OUR ONLINE **Club Chi™**

Even the best dogs have some bad habits. If you are frustrated with a particular behavior that your toy dog exhibits, don't despair! Go online and join Club Chi where you can ask other toy dog owners for advice on dealing with excessive digging, stubbornness, housetraining issues and more. Log on to **DogChannel.com/Club-Chi** and click on "Community."

CHAPTER 11

BREAKING

BAD HABITS

Discipline — training one to act in accordance with rules — brings order to life. It is as simple as that. Without discipline, particularly in a group society, chaos reigns supreme and the group will eventually perish. Humans and canines are social animals and need some form of discipline in order to function effectively. Dogs need discipline in their lives in order to understand how their pack (you and other family members) functions and how they must act in order to survive.

Living with an untrained dog is a lot like owning a piano you don't know how to play; it's a nice object to look at, but it doesn't do much else for you. Now, begin taking piano lessons and suddenly the piano comes alive and brings forth magical sounds that set your heart singing and your body swaying.

The same is true with your Chihuahua. Any dog is a big responsibility, and if not trained, may develop unacceptable behavior that annoy you or could even cause friction in the family.

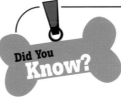

Did You Know?

Anxiety can make a puppy miserable. Living in a world with scary monsters and suspected Chihuahua-eaters roaming the streets has to be pretty nerve-racking. The good news is that timid dogs are not doomed to be forever ruled by fear. Owners who understand a timid Chi's needs can help her build self-confidence and a more optimistic view of life.

STOP THAT WHINING

A puppy will often cry, whine, whimper, howl or make some type of commotion when he is left alone. This is basically his way of calling out for attention, of calling out to make sure that you know he is there and that you have not forgotten about him. He feels insecure when he is left alone; for example, when you are out of the house and he is in his crate, or when you are in another part of the house and he cannot see you. The noise he is making is an expression of the anxiety he feels at being alone, so he needs to be taught that being alone is OK. You are not actually training your dog to stop making noise, you are training him to feel comfortable when he is alone and thus removing the need to make the noise.

This is where the crate with a cozy blanket and a toy comes in handy. You want to know that your puppy is safe when you are not there to supervise, and you know that he will be safe in his crate rather than roaming about the house. In order for the pup to stay in his crate without making a fuss, he needs to be comfortable there. On that note, it is extremely important that his crate is never used as a form of punishment, or your Chihuahua will form a negative association with his crate.

Acclimate your pup to his crate in short, gradually increasing, intervals of time in which you put him in the crate, maybe with a treat, and stay in the room with him. If he cries or makes a fuss, do not go to him, but stay in his sight. Eventually, he will realize that staying in his crate is all right without your help, and it will not be so traumatic for him when you are not around. You may want to leave the radio on softly when you leave the house; the sound of human voices can be comforting.

SMART TIP!

The golden rule of dog training is simple. For each "question" (cue), there is only one correct "answer" (reaction). One cue equals one reaction. Keep practicing the cue until your dog reacts correctly without hesitation. Be repetitive but not monotonous. Dogs get bored just as people do; a bored dog will not be focused on the lesson.

CHEW ON THIS

The national canine pastime is chewing! Every dog loves to sink his "canines" into a tasty bone, but most anything will do. Dogs need to chew to massage their gums, to make their new teeth feel better and to exercise their jaws. This is a natural behavior deeply embedded in all things canine. Our role as owners is not to stop our dog from chewing, but to redirect him to appropriate, chew-worthy objects. Be an informed owner and purchase proper chew toys for your Chihuahua, like strong nylon bones made for mouthy dogs. Be sure that the toys are safe and durable, because your dog's safety is at risk.

The best answer is prevention: That is, put your shoes, handbags and other tasty objects in their proper places (out of the reach of your canine's mouth). Direct puppies to their toys whenever you see them gnawing furniture legs or the leg of your pants. Make a noise to attract your Chihuahua's attention and immediately escort him to his chew toy and engage him with the toy for at least four minutes, praising and encouraging him all the while.

NIP NIPPING

As puppies start to teethe, they feel the need to sink their teeth into everything;

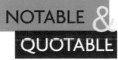
NOTABLE & QUOTABLE

The best way to get through to dogs is through their stomach and mind — not the use of force. You have to play a mind game with them.

— *Sara Gregware, professional dog handler and trainer in Goshen, Conn.*

unfortunately, that includes your fingers, arms, hair, toes, whatever happens to be available. You may find this behavior cute for about the first five seconds — until you feel just how sharp those puppy teeth are.

Nipping is something you want to discourage immediately and consistently with a firm "No!" (or whatever number of firm "Nos" it takes for your dog to understand that you mean business) and replace your finger with an appropriate chew toy.

Nipping seems cute from a puppy, but when an adult nips, it hurts. Don't let a puppy get away with something an adult won't.

UNWANTED BARKING MUST GO

Barking is a dog's way of talking. It can be somewhat frustrating because it is not easy to tell what your dog means by his bark: Is he excited, happy, frightened, angry? Whatever it is that your dog is trying to say, he should not be punished for barking. It is only when the barking becomes excessive and turns into a bad habit, that the behavior needs to be modified.

If an intruder came into your home in the middle of the night and your Chihuahua barked a warning, wouldn't you be pleased? You probably would deem your dog a hero, a wonderful guardian and protector of the home. On the other hand, if a friend drops by unexpectedly and rings the doorbell and is greeted with a sudden sharp bark, you probably would be annoyed. Isn't it just the same behavior? Your dog doesn't know any better — unless he sees who is at the door and it is someone he is familiar with, and he will bark as a means of signaling to you that his (and your) territory is being threatened.

While your friend is not posing a threat, it's all the same to your Chihuahua. Barking is his way of letting you know there is an intruder, whether friend or foe, on your property. This type of barking is instinctive and should not be discouraged.

Excessive habitual barking, however, is a problem that should be corrected early. As your Chi grows up, you will be able to tell when his barking is purposeful and when it is for no reason. You will able to distinguish his different barks and their associations. For example, a Chi's bark will differ when someone is approaching the door from when he is excited to see you. It is similar to a person's tone of voice, except that a dog has to rely totally on tone because he does not have the benefit of using words. An incessant barker will be evident at an early age.

Your Chihuahua may howl, whine or otherwise vocalize her displeasure at your leaving the house and her being left alone. This is a normal case of separation anxiety, but there are things that can be done to eliminate this problem. Your dog needs to learn that she will be fine on her own for a while and that she will not wither away if she isn't attended to every minute of the day.

In fact, constant attention can lead to separation anxiety. If you are endlessly coddling and cuddling your Chihuahua, she will come to expect this behavior from you all of the time, and it will be more traumatic for her when you are not there.

To help minimize separation anxiety, make your entrances and exits as low-key as possible. Do not give your Chi a long, drawn-out good-bye and do not lavish her with hugs and kisses when you return. This will only make her miss you more when you are away.

Another thing you can try is to give your dog a treat when you leave; this will keep her occupied, it will keep her mind off the fact that you just left and it will help her associate your leaving with a pleasant experience.

You may have to acclimate your Chi to being left alone in intervals, much like when you introduced her to her crate. Of course, when your dog starts whimpering as you approach the door, your first instinct will be to run to her and comfort her, but don't do it! Eventually, she will adjust and be just fine if you take it in small steps. Her anxiety stems from being placed in an unfamiliar situation; by familiarizing her with being alone she will learn that she is OK.

When your Chi is alone in the house, confine her in her crate or a designated dog-proof area. This should be the area in which she sleeps, so she will already feel comfortable there and more at ease when she is alone. This is just one of the many examples in which a crate is an invaluable tool for you and your Chihuahua, and reinforces of why your dog should view her crate as a happy place, a place of her own.

SEPARATION ANXIETY

Begging is an art form. Ignore your little artist when he is "performing" or you'll get nightly encores at the dinner table for the rest of his career.

There are some things that encourage a dog to bark. For example, if your dog barks nonstop for a few minutes and you give him a treat to quiet him, he will believe that you are rewarding him for barking. He will associate barking with getting a treat and will keep doing it until he is rewarded.

NO MORE JUMPING

Jumping up is a dog's friendly way of saying hello! Some owners don't mind when their dog jumps up, which is fine for them especially with a dog as small as a Chi. The problem arises when guests arrive and your dog greets them in the same manner — whether they like it or not! However friendly the greeting may be, the chances are your visitors will not appreciate your dog's enthusiasm. Your dog will not be able to distinguish between whom he can jump on and whom he cannot. Therefore, it is probably best to discourage this behavior entirely.

Pick a cue such as "off" (avoid using "down" because you will use that for your dog to lie down) and tell him "off" when he jumps up. Place him on the ground on all fours and have him sit, praising him the whole time. Always lavish him with praise and petting when he is in the sit position. That way you are still giving him a warm affectionate greeting, because you are as pleased to see him as he is to see you!

FOOD STEALING AND BEGGING

Is your dog devising ways to steal food from your cupboards? If so, you must answer these questions: Is your Chihuahua really hungry? Why is there food on the coffee table? Face it, some dogs are more food-motivated than others; some dogs are totally obsessed by a slab of brisket and can only think of their next meal. Food

Most behavioral problems begin in puppyhood. Set the stage for a well-behaved adult the minute you bring your new puppy home.

NOTABLE & QUOTABLE

Stage false departures. Pick up your car keys and put on your coat, then put them away and go about your routine. Do this several times a day, ignoring your dog while you do it. Soon, her reaction to these triggers will decrease.

— September Morn, a dog trainer and behavior specialist in Bellingham, Wash.

stealing is terrific fun and always yields a great reward — food, glorious food!

The owner's goal, therefore, is to make the reward less rewarding, even startling! Plant a shaker can (an empty can filled with coins and a lid on top) on the table so that it catches your pooch off-guard. There are other devices available that will surprise your dog when he is looking for a mid-afternoon snack. Such remote-control devices, though not the first choice of some trainers, allow the correction to come from the object instead of the owner. These devices are also useful to keep the snacking hound from napping on furniture.

Just like food stealing, begging is a favorite pastime of hungry puppies with that same food reward. Dogs quickly learn that humans love that feed-me pose and their selfish owners keep the "good food" for themselves. Why would humans dine on kibble when they can cook up sausages and kielbasa? Begging is a conditioned response related to a specific stimulus, time and place. The sounds of the kitchen, cans and bottles opening, crinkling bags and the smell of food being prepared will excite the chowhound and soon the paws will be in the air!

Here is the solution to stop this behavior: Never give in to a beggar, no matter how cute or desperate! You are rewarding your dog for sitting pretty, jumping up, whining and rubbing his nose into you by giving him that glorious food reward. By ignoring your dog, you will (eventually) force the behavior into extinction. Note that this behavior will likely get worse before it disappears, so be sure there aren't any softies in the family who will give in to your dog when he whimpers, "Pretty please."

DIG THIS

Digging, which is seen as a destructive behavior to humans, is actually quite a natural behavior in dogs and their desire to dig can be irrepressible and frustrating to owners. When digging occurs in your yard, it is actually a normal behavior redirected into something your dog can do in his everyday life. In the wild, a dog would be actively seeking food, making his own shelter, etc. He would be using his paws in a purposeful manner for his survival. Because you provide him with food and shelter, he has no need to use his paws for these purposes, and so the energy that he would be using may manifest itself in the form of little holes all over your yard and flower beds.

Perhaps your dog is

digging as a reaction to boredom — It is somewhat similar to someone eating a whole bag of chips in front of the TV — because they are there and there is nothing better to do! Basically, the answer is to provide your dog with adequate play and exercise so that his mind and paws are occupied, and so that he feels as if he is doing something useful.

Of course, digging is easiest to control if it is stopped as soon as possible, but it is often hard to catch a dog in the act. If your dog is a compulsive digger and is not easily distracted by other activities, you can designate an area on your property where it is OK for him to dig. If you catch him digging in an off-limits area of the yard, immediately bring him to the approved area and praise him for digging there. Keep a close eye on him so you can catch him in the act; that is the only way to make him understand what is permitted and what is not. If you take him to a hole he dug an hour ago and tell him "No," he will understand that you are not fond of holes, dirt, or uprooted flowers. If you catch him while he is deep in your tulips, that is when he will get your message.

POOP ALERT!

Humans find eating feces, aka coprophagia, one of the most disgusting behaviors their dog could engage in; yet to your dog, it is perfectly normal. Vets have found that diets, containing relatively low levels of fiber and high levels of starch, increase the incidence of coprophagia. Therefore, high-fiber diets may decrease the likelihood of dogs eating feces. To discourage this behavior in your Chihuahua, feed him a proper amount of food that is complete and balanced. If changes in his diet do not seem to work, and no medical cause can be found, you will have to modify the behavior

Did You Know? Some natural remedies for separation anxiety are reputed to have calming effects, but check with your vet before use. Flower essence remedies are water-based extracts of different plants, which are stabilized and preserved with alcohol. A human dose is only a few drops, so seek advice from a natural healing practitioner on proper dosage for your Chi.

through environmental control before it becomes a habit.

There are some tricks you can try, such as adding an unsavory substance to the feces to make it unpalatable, or adding something to your dog's food which will make it taste unpleasant after it passes through your dog. The best way to prevent your dog from eating his stool is to make it unavailable; clean up after he eliminates and remove any stool from the yard. If it is not there, he cannot eat it.

Never reprimand your dog for stool eating, as this rarely impresses him. Vets recommend distracting your dog while he is in the act of eating stool. Another option is to muzzle him when he is in the yard to relieve himself; this usually is effective within 30 to 60 days. Coprophagia is most frequently seen in pups 6 to 12 months of age, and usually disappears around the dog's first birthday.

LEASH PULLING

There are actually two types of loose-leash walking. One is "heeling," where the dog is on your left, looking up at you. The other is when your dog can be anywhere as

SMART TIP!

Pushing your Chi puppy to do something she's scared of will only increase her anxiety. Stay within your puppy's emotional comfort zone. A dog expresses emotions with her tail, ears, eyes and mouth. Signs of anxiety or fear include drooped ears, a downward pointing tail and quick panting.

long as the leash is loose. Both styles are fine, and both have their uses. Loose-leash walking is great for trail and potty walks. Heeling is great when you need to get your dog's attention to navigate a narrow spot or pass distractions.

A harness is great for walking a toy dog. Let's face it, small doesn't mean slow. Those tiny little legs are fast! And with that momentum comes jarring whiplash or possible neck or spinal dam

age if they hit the end of the leash at top speed. Harnesses help avoid these potential problems because they take the pressure off your dog's neck.

Use a long leash (15 feet or longer), that way you aren't forcing your dog to walk next to you. It is very important to give your dog the choice to stay with you (or not) but heavily reinforce the correct choice.

Arm yourself with a harness, a long leash and a lot of tiny treats, good stuff like bits of cooked chicken, hot dog or small pieces of cheese. Although the same old dry biscuit may work in your kitchen, you don't need loose-leash walking there. Your dog's paycheck has to be better outside to compete with the outdoors and the temptations they hold.

Before you start, you will need to teach your dog a marker signal — something that tells him when he did a behavior correctly at the exact instant he did it. You can use a clicker or the word "yes." Either click or say your word and instantly give him a treat. Repeat a few minutes per session, a few times per day for about two to three days. By that time he should know that the click or special word means a treat is coming.

Be sure to vary your reinforcement type. "Treat" doesn't have to always be food; you can use belly rubs, head pats, play, toys — whatever your dog likes.

Practice the following steps in many different kinds of locations; start with low-level distractions and gradually increase the intensity.

STEP 1 — PLAY: The first step to teaching loose-leash walking is to simply play with your dog. Fake left and right, race around and every few seconds, click him for staying with you and give him a few treats. Repeat for a few minutes per session, a few times per day. Once your dog realizes how much fun it is to be glued to you and you couldn't get rid of him if you tried, you are ready for the next move.

STEP 2 — BACK UP: While playing, start to walk backward, click as he follows and give him a treat. Change direction frequently and every now and then, go back to play mode; this will encourage your dog to stay with you because you are being more fun. Gradually reduce the play and increase the backing up.

STEP 3 — PIVOT: Place the leash in your right hand, and hold the treats in your left. If you reach around with your right hand to feed him on your left, he will trip you in his attempt to get to your right side. Once your dog is a pro at back-ups, pivot (turn in place to your right) so he is on your left. Click and give him a few treats for each step he is still with you. Then, click and treat when he is looking up at you. Once in a while, play with him again.

Slowly but surely, you can reduce the amount of treats for longer loose-leash walking. Once your dog is staying next to you on a regular basis, you can name this new behavior. The most common words are "heel," "with me" or "strut."

STEP 4 — CHECK IN: Go for a long walk. Let your dog sniff to his heart's content. When he happens to look back at you, click and jackpot! (Tons of tiny treats, all fed one treat at a time). Release him with a verbal

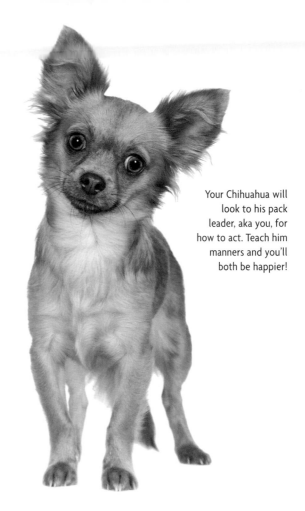

Your Chihuahua will look to his pack leader, aka you, for how to act. Teach him manners and you'll both be happier!

"OK," and continue on your walk. Keep your eyes glued to him; each and every time he "checks in," click and jackpot. You should find that within a very short time, he'll stay right by your side. Click and feed him (and use those other reinforcers) when he is staying next to you. You can name this behavior "let's go," "let's walk" or anything you wish.

STEP 5 — MIX IT UP: Now that your dog knows how to heel and walk on a loose

NOTABLE & QUOTABLE

The purpose of puppy classes is for puppies to learn how to learn. The pups get the training along the way, but the training is almost secondary.
— *professional trainer Peggy Shunick Duezabou of Helena, Mont.*

leash, mix it up. As you are walking, ask your dog to heel and see if he'll move into the heel position. If he does, click and treat (a lot!). Continue to click and treat for a few steps and then release him to continue on with his loose-leash walk. Periodically call him back to you to heel and then let him go again. Pretty soon you'll have a dog who loves to walk on a loose-leash and you will be the envy of all your neighbors — especially those who thought toy dogs couldn't be trained!

SEXUAL BEHAVIOR

Dogs exhibit certain sexual behaviors that may have influenced your choosing a male or female when you purchased your Chihuahua. Spaying/neutering will eliminate most of these behaviors, but if you are purchasing a dog who you wish to show or breed, you should be aware of what you will have to deal with during the dog's life.

Females usually have two estruses (heat cycles) per year, each cycle lasting about three weeks. These are the only times in which she will mate, and she usually will not allow this until the second week. If she is not bred during the heat cycle, it is not uncommon for her to experience a false pregnancy, in which her mammary glands swell and she exhibits maternal tendencies toward her toys.

Owners must recognize that mounting, a common behavior, is not merely a sexual expression but also a way of displaying dominance. Be consistent as well as persistent, and you will find that you can "move mounters."

CAT INTRODUCTIONS

Cats are the pet most likely to arouse your puppy's interest. Besides all the other reasons you shouldn't let your puppy have run of the house, your cat is yet another. This is

your cat's house, and cats are very territorial, and having a puppy invade your cat's territory isn't going to make things easier. When you do start letting your puppy see more of the house, keep him on a leash and don't let him get into the cat's special places.

Your puppy is likely to want to play with your cat, and your cat is likely to not find this one bit amusing. If the puppy rushes at the cat, or even sniffs too brazenly, the pup is likely to get a swat in the face with some sharp claws. Although that may quickly teach him the hazards of cat chasing, it does so with the risk of a scratched eye. And if the

cat runs, that's so rewarding to the puppy that he's likely to do it again.

Your best bet is to train both pets to coexist, and the best way to do that at first is to keep one in a crate while you train the other. Then take turns and have them trade places. Feed them next to each other or reward them with special treats for ignoring one another. Don't rush. You have years for them to be buddies, but you can sabotage it in days if you let things get out of hand.

Some older cats will remain snooty. You'll need to protect your puppy if your cat is the attacking type, but don't let your cat win by removing your puppy from the room. When your cat is the one with the bad manners, he is the one who should have to leave the room. You don't want him to learn that beating up your puppy gets rid of the little trespasser.

And don't force them to be together if they don't want to. They will eventually work out a comfortable distance for each of them. Many cats and dogs grow to be close pals, while others prefer to look at each other from afar. The younger both are when you bring them home to be fast, and furry, friends.

Dogs and cats don't have to be enemies. Introduce them properly, and they'll be best buds for life.

CHAPTER 12

SPORTS

FOR TOYS

Your Chihuahua may look like little more than a miniscule, movable ball of fur with bright, shiny eyes, but don't let his small size fool you. There's a whole lot of energy in this toy that needs some fun and excitement.

EXERCISE OPTIONS

All dogs need exercise to keep them physically and mentally healthy. An inactive dog is an unfit dog, with the accompanying risk of joint strain or torn ligaments. Inactive dogs are also prone to mischief and may do anything to relieve their boredom. This often leads to behavioral problems, such as chewing or barking. Regular daily exercise, such as daily walks and play sessions, will help keep your Chihuahua slim, trim and perfectly happy.

Provide your Chi with interactive play that stimulates his mind and body. It's a good idea to have a daily period of one-on-one play time, especially with a puppy or young dog. Continue this type of interaction throughout your dog's life, and you will build a lasting bond. Even seniors who are slowing down a bit need to perform stimulating activities.

If your Chi is older or overweight, consult your veterinarian about how much, and what type, of exercise he needs. Usually, a 10- to 15-minute walk once a day is a good

Did You Know? The Fédération Internationale Cynologique is the world kennel club that governs dog shows around the world.

SMART TIP!

Before You Begin
Because of the physical demands of dog sports, a Chihuahua puppy should not officially begin training until she is done growing. That doesn't mean that you can't begin socializing her to sports, though. Talk to your vet about what age is appropriate to begin more intense training.

start. As the pounds start to drop off, your dog's energy level will rise, and you can increase his amount of daily exercise.

Whether a dog is trained in the structured environment of a class or alone with his owner at home, there also are many sporting activities that can bring fun and rewards to you and your dog once you have mastered basic training techniques.

OBEDIENCE TRIALS

Obedience trials in the United States trace back to the early 1930s, when organized obedience training was developed to demonstrate how well dog and owner could work together. The pioneer of obedience trials was Helen Whitehouse Walker, a Standard Poodle fancier, who designed a series of exercises after the Associated Sheep, Police and Army Dog Society of Great Britain. Since then, obedience trials have grown by leaps and bounds, and today more than 2,000 trials are held in the United States every year, with more than 100,000 dogs competing. Any registered American Kennel Club or United Kennel Club dog can enter an obedience trial for the club in which he is registered, regardless of conformational disqualifications or neutering.

Obedience trials are divided into three levels of progressive difficulty. At the Novice level, dogs compete for the title of Companion Dog; at the Open level, dogs compete for a Companion Dog Excellent title; and at the Advanced level, dogs compete for a Utility Dog title. Classes are subdivided into "A" (for beginners) and "B" (for more experienced handlers). A perfect score at any level is 200, and a dog must score 170 or better to earn a "leg," of three which are needed to earn the title. To earn points, the dog must score more than 50 percent of the available points in each exercise; the possible points range from 20 to 40.

Once a dog has earned the UD title, he can compete with other proven obedience dogs for the coveted title of Utility Dog Excellent, which requires that the dog win "legs" in 10 shows. In 1977, the title Obedience Trial Champion was established by the AKC. Utility Dogs who earn legs in Open B and Utility B earn points toward their Obedience Trial Champion title. To become an OTCh., a dog needs to earn 100 points, which requires three first places in Open B and Utility under three different judges.

The Grand Prix of obedience trials, the AKC National Obedience Invitational, gives qualifying Utility Dogs the chance to win the newest and highest title: National Obedience Champion. Only the top 25 ranked obedience dogs, plus any dog ranked in the top three in his breed, are allowed to compete.

AGILITY TRIALS

Agility is one of the most popular dog sports out there. Training your Chihuahua in agility will boost his confidence and teach him to focus on you.

In agility competition, Chihuahua and handler move through a prescribed course, maneuvering through a series of obstacles that may include jumps, tunnels, a dog walk, an A-frame, a seesaw, a pause table and

Did You Know? **Agility was initially designed for medium-sized breeds,** so it's not surprising that some obstacles present special challenges for diminutive dogs. The teeter-totter is probably the scariest and most difficult obstacle, because it tips and sinks under the dog, then hits the ground with a bang. That drop and sudden stop can be uncomfortable and can even bounce off a small dog. The plank end, hitting the ground and making a startling "bang," also distracts many small dogs.

SMART TIP!

Sports are physically demanding. Have your vet do a full examination of your Chihuahua to rule out joint problems, heart disease, eye ailments and other maladies. Once you get health clearance, start having fun in your new dog-sporting life!

weave poles. Dogs who run through a course without refusing any obstacles, going off course or knocking down any bars, all within a set time, get a qualifying score. Dogs with a certain number of qualifying scores in their given division (Novice, Open, Excellent and Mach, at AKC trials) earn an agility title.

Several different organizations recognize agility events. AKC-sanctioned agility events are the most common. The United States Dog Agility Association also sanctions agility trials, as does the UKC. The rules are different for each of these organizations, but the principles are the same.

When your Chihuahua starts his agility training, he will begin by learning to negotiate each individual obstacle while on leash, as you guide him. Eventually, you will steer him through a few obstacles in a row, one after another. Once he catches on that this is how agility works, he can run a short course off leash. One day, you'll see the light go on in your Chihuahua's eyes as he figures out that he should look to you for guidance as he runs through the agility course. Your job will be to tell him which obstacles to take next, using voice and your body as signals.

RALLY BEHIND RALLY

Rally is a sport that combines competition obedience with elements of agility but is less demanding than either one of these activi-

ties. Rally was designed keeping the average dog owner in mind and is easier than many other sporting activities.

At a rally event, dogs and handlers are asked to move through 10 to 20 different stations, depending on the level of competition. The stations are marked by numbered signs, which tell the handler the exercise to be performed at each station. The exercises vary from making different types of turns to changing pace.

Dogs can earn rally titles as they get better at the sport and move through the different levels. The titles to strive for are Rally Novice, Rally Advanced, Rally Excellent and Rally Advanced Excellent.

To get your Chihuahua puppy prepared to do rally competition, focus on teaching him basic obedience, for starters. Your dog must know the five basic obedience cues — sit, down, stay, come and heel — and perform them well before he's ready for rally. Next, you can enroll your dog in a rally class. Although he must be at least 6 months of age to compete in rally, you can start training long before his 6-month birthday.

FLYBALL

In the canine relay race of flyball, four straight-line hurdles lead to a box that ejects a tennis ball after impact on the release pedal. Hurdles are set at a height appropriate for the shortest dog (probably your Chihuahua) on a team of four. Ideally, each dog leaps the hurdles, runs to the box, jumps on the pedal, catches the tennis ball in his mouth and repeats his path back to the waiting handler, cueing the next dog's release.

Flyball training may be difficult to find in some areas, though training clubs and private trainers certainly warrant an inquiring phone call. Should this route prove fruitless, purchase flyball equipment and start your own team!

Chihuahuas are great team players. Get them on a flyball team and watch them fly!

MUSICAL FREESTYLE

A stunning combination of obedience, tricks and dance, freestyle is the perfect venue for those possessing an artistic flair. Set within a large, open ring, a handler and dog perform a personally choreographed routine in rhythm to their choice of music. A typical presentation might find a dog weaving between the handler's legs as he or she is walking, spinning in place, doing leg kicks and other imaginative moves. Creative handler costumes and fancy dog collars often complete the picture.

Most participants agree that dogs display preferences in music, responding happily to tunes they like while ignoring those they don't. Debora Wheeler of Gilmanton, N.H., says her Chihuahua, Cain, enjoys musical freestyle training. "He's a happy little dog that loves to perform," she says.

If you're worried about your own dance skills, self choreography allows you to focus on your team's special talents. Find the ham in your little Chihuahua at a local training facility or private trainer. Alternatively, contact the sport's host organizations, the Canine Freestyle Federation and the World Canine Freestyle Organization for information about getting your start in this exciting activity.

SMART TIP!

Safety is another agility challenge for a toy dog. Contact obstacles like the teeter, dogwalk and A-frame place dogs two to six feet off the ground. A fall from that height can injure any dog, and for a toy breed, it's a proportionally longer fall. When first training on contact obstacles, have a spotter on the opposite side of your dog if possible, in case she loses his balance.

SHOW DOGS

When you purchase your Chihuahua puppy, make it clear to the breeder whether you want one just as a lovable companion and pet, or if you hope to be buying a Chihuahua with show prospects. No reputable breeder will sell you a puppy and tell you the dog will definitely be show quality because so much can change during the early months of a puppy's development. If you do plan to show, what you hopefully will have acquired is a puppy with show "potential."

To the novice, exhibiting a Chihuahua in the ring may look easy, but it takes a lot of hard work and devotion to win at a show such as the Westminster Kennel Club dog show, not to mention a little luck, too!

The first thing the canine novice learns when watching a dog show is that each dog first competes against members of his own breed. Once the judge has selected the best member of each breed (Best of Breed) the chosen dog will compete with other dogs in his group. Finally, the dogs chosen first in each group will compete for Best in Show.

The second concept that you must understand is that the dogs are not compared against one another. The judge compares each dog against the breed standard, the written description of the ideal specimen approved by the AKC or UKC, depending on the sponsoring club. While some early breed standards were based on famous or popular dogs, many dedicated enthusiasts say that a perfect specimen as described in the standard has never walked into a show ring, has never been bred and, to the woe of dog breeders around the globe, does not exist. Breeders attempt to get as close to this ideal as possible with every litter, but theoretically the "perfect" dog is so elusive that it is impos-

NOTABLE & QUOTABLE

Asking a Chihuahua to go over the A-frame is like asking him to climb a mountain and slide down the other side. It takes courage, self confidence and determination to make it up and over.

— agility competitor and Chi owner Judy Petersen, of Kasota, Minn.

it's a Fact

The Teacup Dogs Agility Association was formed to provide a competition venue for small dogs. Dogs of any breed or mix are welcomed in TDAA competitions — as long as they're not taller than 17 inches at the shoulder. Visit www.k9tdaa.com for more information.

sible. (And if the perfect dog were born, breeders and judges probably would never agree that he was perfect.)

If you are interested in exploring the world of conformation, your best bet is to join your local or national (or parent) breed club, the Chihuahua Dog Club of America. These clubs often host regional and national specialties, shows only for Chihuahuas, which can include conformation as well as obedience trials. Even if you have no intention of competing with your Chihuahua, a specialty is a like a festival for lovers of the breed who congregate to share their favorite topic: Chihuahuas! Clubs also send out newsletters and some organize training days and seminars so people can learn more about Chis. To locate the breed club closest to you, contact the AKC or UKC, which furnishes the rules and regulations for all of these events, general dog registration and other basic requirements of dog ownership.

THERAPY DOGS

Therapy work offers a special kind of satisfaction, the gratification of bringing pleasure simply through your dog's presence. If you like helping people, you and your Chihuahua can bring happiness and laughter to people who are confined to hospitals and nursing homes. Therapy-dog visits are a wonderful way for you to share the joys of owning a Chihuahua. Petting your dog can ease the loneliness of a widower in a nursing home, lower the blood pressure of a hospital patient and win big grins and laughs from children in a cancer ward.

Your therapy Chihuahua must be clean, flea-free and exhibit good manners. No food stealing or potty accidents! He must pass a temperament test to ensure that he's suited for this type of work. A sweet, tolerant, fearless disposition is ideal because therapy work involves encounters with new or unusual places, people and equipment. Both of you will attend training classes before visits begin. Be sure to take normal precautions against falls from aged, shaky hands or run-ins with wheelchairs or walkers. A short leash attached to a harness will help you keep control.

CANINE GOOD CITIZEN

If obedience work sounds too regimented but you'd still like your Chihuahua to have a title, prepare him for the Canine Good Citizen test. This program is sponsored by the AKC with tests administered by local dog clubs, private trainers and 4-H clubs.

To earn a CGC title, your Chi must be well-groomed and demonstrate the manners that all good dogs should exhibit. The CGC test requires a dog to perform the sit, down, stay, and come cues; react appropriately to other dogs and distractions; allow a stranger to approach him; sit politely for petting; walk nicely on a loose lead; move through a crowd without going wild; calm down after play or praise and sit still for examination by the judge. Find out more at DogChannel. com/Club-Chi — click on "Downloads."

162 | CHIHUAHUA

Don't let your Chihuahua sit around wishing he could get in on the action. Get involved in a dog sport today!

True Tails

Protecting your little guy from the big guys

Your Chihuahua will probably be the smallest dog in your agility training class. Many dogs aren't familiar with toy breeds and react as if Chihuahuas are prey. A large, excited dog pouncing on your Chi could cause serious injuries before anyone could intervene, so make sure that while your Chi is running, all larger dogs are securely held by their handlers, tethered to something immovable, or crated. When large dogs are off-leash, either crate your Chi or hold her in your arms.

Judy Petersen, of Kasota, Minn., suggests finding a class with enough room in the training ring so you can stand back while other dogs run. "The instructor needs to appreciate small dogs and be aware of the danger they can be in from larger dogs." Petersen says. Petersen owns Doberman Pinschers as well as Chihuahuas, and she is very careful with her little guys. "I have shown Chis for six years and you get used to watching out for other dogs," she says. "When Lenny runs, he'll be in my arms until we go into the ring, and I'll have some friends at the exit to make sure it's safe."

Chrissie Brounell of Andover, N.J., has had several experiences with larger dogs attacking her Chihuahua during agility class. She recommends asking the following safety-related questions when evaluating schools:

■ Are the dogs required to have obedience training?

■ What is the policy regarding dogs who lunge at other dogs?

■ What is the policy regarding owners who can't control their dogs off-leash?

■ Are dogs crated or leashed during other dogs' runs?

■ How many toy dogs have successfully trained in your classes?

■ Have the other students been told there will be a toy dog in class?

Dog shows are fun to watch, and even more fun to participate in.

CHAPTER 13

RESOURCES

To find out more information about Chihuahuas, contact the following organizations. They will be glad to help you dig deeper into the world of this toy breed.

American Kennel Club: The AKC website offers information and links to conformation, rally, obedience and agility programs and member clubs. www.akc.org

Association of Pet Dog Trainers: If you are looking for a great trainer, start here. www.apdt.com

Canadian Kennel Club: Our northern neighbor's oldest kennel club is similar to the AKC. www.ckc.ca

Chihuahua Club of America: This is the AKC-recognized, national breed club. www.chihuahuaclubofamerica.com

Love on a Leash: There are more than 900 members of this pet therapy organization. www.loveonaleash.org

North American Dog Agility Council: This site provides links to clubs, events and agility trainers in the United States and Canada. www.nadac.com

North American Flyball Association: This growing all-breed sport combines racing, tennis-ball fetching and fun. www.flyball.org

it's a **Fact** The **American Kennel Club** was started in 1884. It is America's oldest kennel club. The **United Kennel Club** is the second oldest in the United States. It began registering dogs in 1898.

Therapy Dogs Inc.: Get your Chi involved in therapy. www.therapydogs.com

Therapy Dogs International: Find more therapy dog info here: www.tdi-dog.org

United Kennel Club: The UKC offers several of the events offered by the AKC, including agility, conformation and obedience. The UKC also offers competitions for other sports. Both the UKC and the AKC offer programs for juniors, ages 2 to 18. www.ukcdogs.com

United States Dog Agility Association: This organization offers information about agility training, local clubs and local and national events in the United States, Canada and Mexico, as well as overseas. www.usdaa.com

World Canine Freestyle Organization: With a little bit of training, cleverly matching costumes and some music, you'll be dancing with your Chihuahua in no time. www.worldcaninefreestyle.org

BOARDING

So you want to take a family vacation, and you want to include all members of the family. You usually make arrangements ahead of time anyway, but this is imperative when traveling with a Chihuahua. You do not want to make an overnight stop at the only place around for miles and find out the hotel doesn't allow dogs. Also, you do not want to reserve a room for your family without confirming that you are traveling with a dog, because if it is against the hotel's policy, you may not have a place to stay.

Alternatively, if you are traveling and choose not to bring your Chihuahua, you will have to make arrangements for him. Some options are to bring him to a family member or a neighbor, have a trusted friend stop by often, stay at your house or bring your dog to a reputable boarding kennel.

If you choose to board him at a kennel, visit in advance to see the facilities and check how clean they are and where the dogs are kept. Talk to some of the employees and see how they treat the dogs; do they spend time with the dogs, play with them, exercise them, etc.? Also, find out the kennel's policy on vaccinations and what they require. This is for all of the dogs' safety because when dogs are kept together, there is a greater risk of diseases being passed from dog to dog.

HOME STAFFING

For the Chihuahua owner who works during the day or finds himself away from home on certain days, a pet sitter or dog walker may be the perfect solution for a lonely toy dog longing for a midday stroll. Smart dog owners can approach local high schools or community centers if they can't find a neighbor interested in a part-time commitment. Interview potential dog walkers and consider their experience with dogs, as well as your Chihuahua's rapport with the candidate. (Chihuahuas are excellent judges of character!) Always check references before entrusting your toy dog and home to a new dog walker.

For an owner's long-term absence, such as a business trip or vacation, many Chihuahua owners welcome the services of a pet sitter. It's usually less stressful on your dog to stay home with a pet sitter than to be boarded in a kennel. Pet sitters also may be more affordable than a week's stay at a full-service doggie day care.

Pet sitters must be even more reliable than dog walkers because your dog will be depending on his surrogate owner for all of his needs for an extended period. Smart owners are advised to hire a certified pet sitter through the National Association of Professional Pet Sitters, which can be accessed online at www.petsitters.org. NAPPS

provides online and toll-free pet sitter locator services. The nonprofit organization certifies serious-minded, professional individuals who are knowledgeable in canine behavior, nutrition, health and safety. If you always consider your Chi's best interest at heart when planning a trip, you'll be rewarding with peace of mind while away.

SCHOOL'S IN SESSION

Puppy kindergarten, which is usually open to puppies between 3 to 6 months, allows puppies to learn and socialize with other dogs and people in a structured setting. Classes help your Chihuahua enjoy going places with you and help your dog become a well-behaved member at public gatherings that include other dogs. They prepare him for adult obedience classes, as well as for life.

The problem with most puppy kindergarten classes is that most are held only one night a week. What about during the rest of the week?

If you're at home all week, you may be able to find other places to take your puppy, but you have to be careful about dog parks and other places where just any dog can go. An experience with a bully can undo all the good your classes have done, or worse, end in tragedy.

If you work, your puppy may be home alone all day, a tough situation for Chihuahua. Chances are he can't hold his urine in for that long, so your potty training will be undermined unless you're just aiming to teach him to use an indoor potty. And chances are, by the time you come home, he'll be bursting with energy, and you may start to think he's hyperactive.

The answer for the professional with a Chihuahua is doggie day care. Most larger cities have some sort of day care, whether it's a boarding kennel that keeps your dog in a run or a full-service day care that offers training, play time and even spa facilities. They range from a person who keeps a few dogs at his home to a state-of-the-art facility just for dogs. Many of the more sophisticated doggie day cares offer webcams so you can see your dog throughout the day. Here are some things to look for:

- escape-proof facilities, including a buffer between the dogs and any doors
- inoculation requirements for new dogs
- midday meals for young dogs
- obedience training using reward-based methods
- safe and comfortable sleeping areas
- screening dogs for aggression
- small groups of similar sizes and ages
- toys and playground equipment
- trained staff, with an adequate number to supervise the dogs (no more than 10 to 15 dogs per person)
- a webcam

Remember to keep your Chihuahua's leash slack when interacting with other dogs. It is not unusual for a toy dog to pick out one or two canine neighbors to dislike. If you know there's bad blood, step off to the side and put a barrier, such as a parked car, between the dogs. If there are no barriers to be had, move to the side of the walkway, cue your dog to sit, stay and watch you until her nemesis passes; then continue your walk.

SMART TIP!

CAR TRAVEL

You should acclimate your Chi to riding in a car at an early age. You may or may not plan to take him in the car often, but who are we kidding? Of course, you will! At the very least, he will need to go to the vet and you do not want these trips to be traumatize your dog or be troublesome for you. The safest way for your dog to ride in the car is in his crate. If he uses a crate in the house, you can use the same crate for travel.

Another option for your portable Chi is a specially made safety harness for dogs, which straps your toy dog in the car, much like a seat belt. Do not let your dog roam loose in the vehicle or ride in your lap: This

Chihuahuas love road trips! Whether you have an RV or a compact car, taking your Chihuahua with you on vacations makes for memorable holidays.

is very dangerous! If you should stop abruptly, your dog can be thrown and injured. If your dog starts climbing on you and pestering you while you are driving, you will not be able to concentrate on the road. It is an unsafe situation for everyone — human and canine alike. For long trips, stop often to let your Chi relieve himself. Take along whatever you need to clean up after him, including some paper towels should he have an accident in the car or suffer from motion sickness.

IDENTIFICATION

Your Chihuahua is your valued companion and friend. That is why you always keep a close eye on him and you have made sure that he cannot escape from the yard or wriggle out of his collar and run away. However, accidents can happen and there may come a time when your dog unexpectedly gets separated from you. If this should occur, the first thing on your mind will be finding him. Proper identification, including an ID tag, a tattoo and possibly a microchip will increase the chances of his being returned to you safely and quickly.

An ID tag on a collar or harness is the primary means of pet identification (ID licenses are required in many communities). Although inexpensive and easy to read, collars and ID tags can come off or be removed too easily.

A microchip doesn't get lost. Containing a unique ID number that can be read by scanners, the microchip is embedded underneath a dog's skin. It's invaluable for identifying lost or stolen pets. However, to be effective, the microchip must be registered in a national database, and smart owners will be sure their contact info is kept up-to-date.

Additionally, not every shelter or veterinary clinic has a scanner, nor do most folks who might pick up and try to return a lost dog his owner.

Your best bet is to get both!

> **Some communities have created regular dog runs and separate spaces for small dogs.** These dog runs are ideal for introducing puppies to the dog park experience. The runs and participants are smaller and their owners are often more vigilant because they are used to watching out for their fragile companions.
>
> Did You **Know?**

INDEX

CHIHUAHUA, a Smart Owner's Guide™

part of the Kennel Club Books® Interactive Series™

LIBRARY OF CONGRESS CATALOGING-IN-PUBLICATION DATA

Chihuahua / from the editors of Dog fancy magazine.
    p. cm. — (Smart owner's guide)
  Includes bibliographical references and index.
  ISBN 978-1-59378-764-6
  1. Chihuahua (Dog breed) I. Dog fancy (San Juan Capistrano, Calif.)

  SF429.C45C45 2009
  636.76—dc22

                            2009029016

JOIN
Club Chi™
TODAY!